HIKEABLE SEGMENTS

OF THE

NORTH COUNTRY NATIONAL SCENIC TRAIL

Lowell, Michigan 49331

First Edition

The information in this guide is the result of the best effort
of the publisher, using information available at the time of printing.
Changes resulting from maintenance and relocation are constantly
occurring, and, therefore, no published route can be regarded as
precisely accurate at the time you read this notice.

For information, contact:
North Country Trail Association
229 East Main Street
Lowell, Michigan 49331
(888) 454-NCTA
www.northcountrytrail.org
HQ@northcountrytrail.org

ISBN 0-9747280-0-4

Forward

This is the first edition of our new publication, <u>Hikeable Segments of the North Country National Scenic Trail</u>. Many volunteers from across the trail helped us assemble and proof the information in this booklet, and we would especially like to thank Ginny Wanty and Jennifer Tripp for their persistence and dedication to the project. Because we plan to revise and reprint this booklet regularly, we welcome all corrections and any suggestions you may have on how to improve its content and usefulness. To provide comments, please e-mail North Country Trail Association headquarters at HQ@northcountrytrail.org, call us at 888-454-NCTA, or fax your notes to 616-897-6605.

We hope you enjoy our new publication and your journeys on the North Country Trail!

Contents

Frequently Asked Questions

Where does the North Country Trail go?

The North Country National Scenic Trail (NCT) crosses seven states, stretching from the eastern border of New York at Crown Point, to Lake Sakakawea in central North Dakota. Along the way, the trail winds through western Pennsylvania; along the southern perimeter of Ohio; through lower Michigan and across the Mackinac Bridge to the state's Upper Peninsula; across northern Wisconsin; and into the arrowhead, central and western regions of Minnesota.

How long is the Trail? How much is completed?

We expect the trail will total more than 4,000 miles when completed. To date, more than one third of the trail has been "certified" by the National Park Service and many more miles are on the ground and ready to use. Though some people imagine that we're starting at one end and working across the country to complete the NCT, we're actually working to establish new trail nearly everywhere along the corridor. Our challenge now is to connect all the trail segments that already are on the ground.

What's the difference between "certified" trail and trail that isn't?

If a segment of the NCT has been certified by the National Park Service, it means that the trail has been built to certain standards and that someone or some entity has agreed to continually maintain the trail to those standards. The standards involve criteria like marking and signage, vegetation clearing, slope, and allowable uses. A lot of good, off-road segments are not certified for one reason or another but still provide high quality, enjoyable opportunities.

How do I know where the trail is?

Certified segments of the trail are marked at road crossings with the triangular emblem of the trail, which features a white and gold star on a blue field. The trail also is "blazed" to mark it's location. Mostly, blazes are blue rectangles about 2" x 6" that are painted on trees every hundred yards or so. In some areas, the style of blazing varies. White rectangles or blue diamonds may be local variations. If you see two blazes with one offset above the other, this indicates a turn in the trail that may not otherwise be obvious.

Is the NCT a pedestrian only trail, or are other types of uses allowed too?

By federal law, motorized vehicles are not allowed on the trail. Beyond this, our vision is for the trail to provide premier hiking and backpacking experiences, so pedestrian use is the primary "purpose" of the trail. Other types of uses such as mountain bikes or horses, may be allowed on certain trail segments. The decision to allow or prohibit these other types of uses rests with the agency or individual that owns or manages each piece of property the trail crosses.

Can I camp along the trail?
Are there shelters along the trail?

Policies on camping vary according to the land being crossed by the trail. Your best bet is to check with the contacts provided for the segment you are thinking about hiking. Shelters are sparse, but some are available. Again, checking with the Local Information is a good bet. Information on camping and other policies also can be found on trail maps.

Maps? Did you say "maps"? I like maps. Tell me more.

This book lists the maps that are available for each segment of trail, as well as the sources to acquire them. The Hutchins Guidebooks sold by the North Country Trail Association (NCTA) are booklets consisting of hike narratives with hand-drawn maps of the trail. The Johnson maps, also sold by NCTA, are booklets that include basic trail information and black and white maps at varying scales. Other NCTA maps are full-color topographic maps. Maps with a two-letter and two-number code (MI-11) are 1:100,000-scale and maps with an "M" and three numbers (M401) are 1:24,000-scale.

Finger Lakes Trail Conference (FLTC) maps are one-page maps with mileage figures and text on the reverse. Some 3-color maps with topography are available. Buckeye Trail Association (BTA) maps are durable, waterproof, 2-color maps that also provide mileage and other information. Superior Hiking Trail Association (SHTA) topographic pocket-sized maps feature the trail, parking areas, campsites, access roads, and mileages between trailheads. McKenzie maps are 25 x 28-37 inches and are topographically enhanced. Rovers Outing Club maps are black and white topographic maps and include features such as campsites and overlooks.

There's some good information in the Hikeable Segments of the North Country National Scenic Trail, but where can I go for more?

Our website is loaded with all sorts of information about the trail and the organization. You also can buy maps, books and other items there or learn about local Chapters, events and volunteering. You'll find it all at www.northcountrytrail.org.

Who can I contact if I want to know about trail conditions in a particular section?

Some of this information can be found on the website. You also can use the contacts provided in the Hikeable Segments of the North Country National Scenic Trail or online.

Has anyone walked the whole Trail yet?

Ah, there's another reason to visit the website! Yes, several people have and you'll find some of their stories online. Unlike the Appalachian Trail, the NCT runs mainly east-west. Also, it's about twice as long as the "AT," or will be when it's complete. Our website also provides some tips on how to take on this huge challenge. A number of people currently are walking the trail or significant portions of it in bits and pieces.

Who "owns" it? Who is making it happen?

Back in 1980, the U.S. Congress authorized the NCT as part of the National Trails System, and assigned the National Park Service (NPS) to administer it. The NPS only has a couple of employees dedicated to this Herculean task, so most of the "on the ground" work is handled by cooperating agencies, nonprofit organizations and clubs. The North Country Trail Association has about two dozen local Chapters working on the trail, and serves as the lead nonprofit for the entire trail, assisting the NPS in coordinating and facilitating the work of all the other public and private partners.

So, the NPS administers the trail, but who actually owns the land crossed by the NCT?

The NCT traverses a variety of ownerships including a National Park, 10 National Forests, many state and local forests and parks, and private land. When crossing private land, it is especially important to respect the property of these generous landowners who allow the trail to cross their land. It only takes one disrespectful person to prompt a landowner to withdraw permission for the trail to cross, leaving an unwanted gap in the trail.

Does the NCTA need new members? How can I join? How can I find out if there is a chapter near me? If I do join the national organization, will any of my dues help support a local organization?

Absolutely! We welcome new members and rely on their support to build, maintain and protect the North Country Trail. The Hikeable Segments of the North Country National Scenic Trail is provided free of charge to new members, so if you're already a new member, "Welcome!" If not, we hope you'll consider joining. You can do so online (www.northcountrytrail.org), by phone (888-454-NCTA), or through the mail with a membership form. You also may call or write us to request an information packet to review before making a decision. Members may choose to be affiliated with a local NCTA Chapter. When they do this, 25% of their dues go directly to the Chapter. In addition, 12% of all dues are used for grants to our volunteers and partners for on-the-ground trail projects in all seven states.

How can I contact the NCTA or NPS?

NCTA
229 East Main St
Lowell, MI 49331
888-454-6282
HQ@northcountrytrail.org
www.northcountrytrail.org

NPS
700 Rayovac Drive, Ste 100
Madison, WI 53711
608-441-5610
www.nps.gov/noco

New York

The North Country Trail begins at Crown Point State Historic Site on the shore of Lake Champlain. The trail will head west in the 6-million-acre Adirondack Park with its lakes and streams nestled among forested mountains. Outstanding experiences await the hiker in this remote and primitive region. From Boonville, the proposed trail route follows the course of the Old Black River Canal to Rome and Fort Stanwix National Monument, a reconstructed Revolutionary War fort. Leaving Rome, the trail will follow the towpath trail in Old Erie Canal State Park. At Canastota the certified trail continues southward toward Cortland. The trail begins its westward course by following 390 miles of the Finger Lakes Trail. The rolling glacial topography of the Finger Lakes Region provides a scenic setting for the trail with numerous vistas of distant hills and valleys. Along the trail are colorful gorges and plunging waterfalls in a series of state parks. The trail continues through Allegany State Park before leaving the state.

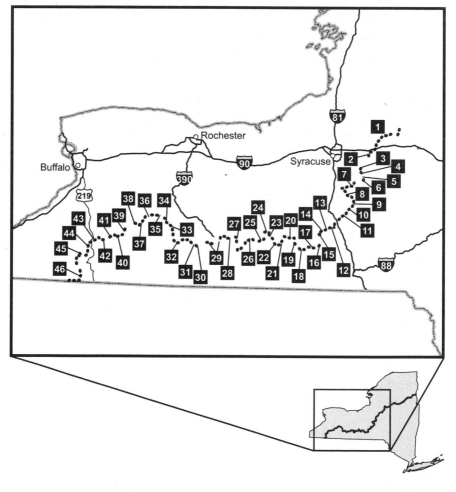

Stone Quarry Hill Art Park
Photo by Central New York Chapter

Tioughnioga Wildlife
Management Area
Photo by Central New York Chapter

Segment 1: Rome to Canastota –
Old Erie Canal State Historic Park

Range: Erie Canal Village in Rome to State Highway 31 in State Bridge
Total Trail Miles: 11.5
Road Walk to Next Segment: 2.2 miles (not blazed)

Range: State Highway 46 in Durhamville to Canal Town Museum in Canastota
Total Trail Miles: 5.2

Local Volunteer Group: Central New York Chapter of NCTA
   www.northcountrytrail.org/cny/index.htm

Local Information: Canal Office, 315-687-7821

Map Sources: NCTA, *Rome to Finger Lakes Trail (NY-04)*

Segment 2: Link Trail

Range: Old Erie Canal State Park in Canastota to Nelson Road west of the Canastota Reservoir

Total Trail Miles: 3.3

Local Volunteer Group: Central New York Chapter of NCTA
www.northcountrytrail.org/cny/index.htm

Map Sources: NCTA, *Rome to Finger Lakes Trail (NY-04)*

Road Walk to Next Segment: 7.2 miles (not blazed)

Segment 3: Link Trail/Gorge Trail

Range: Carey Hill Road to William Street in Cazenovia

Total Trail Miles (Partially Certified): 3.9

Local Volunteer Group: Central New York Chapter of NCTA
www.northcountrytrail.org/cny/index.htm

Map Sources: NCTA, *Rome to Finger Lakes Trail (NY-04)*

Segment 4: Link Trail

Range: William Street in Cazenovia to Constine Bridge Road (southeast of Cazenovia)

Features: Stone Quarry Hill Art Park

Total Trail Miles (Certified): 3.1

Local Volunteer Group: Central New York Chapter of NCTA
www.northcountrytrail.org/cny/index.htm

Map Sources: NCTA, *Rome to Finger Lakes Trail (NY-04)*

Road Walk to Next Segment: 1.2 miles (not blazed)

Labrador Hollow
Photo by Aaron Phipps

Segment 5: Nelson Swamp State Unique Area/Link Trail

Range: Constine Bridge Road (southeast of Cazenovia) to Hardscrabble Road, east of Constine Bridge. *(Note: This segment crosses some private land.)*

Total Trail Miles (Certified): 1.6

Features: Cedar swamp, wealth of flora species, popular bird watching spot, and has what may be the oldest living white pine tree in the eastern US. Interpretive trail loops from main trail.

Local Volunteer Group: Central New York Chapter of NCTA www.northcountrytrail.org/cny/index.htm

Map Sources: NCTA, *Rome to Finger Lakes Trail (NY-04)*

Road Walk to Next Segment: 1 mile (blazed)

Segment 6: Tioughnioga Wildlife Management Area

Range: Irish Hill Road to Holmes Road (southwest of Constine Bridge)

Features: Nesting ponds for waterfowl as well as numerous cleared areas to provide a varied habitat for wildlife.

Total Trail Miles (Certified): 0.6

Local Volunteer Group: Central New York Chapter of NCTA www.northcountrytrail.org/cny/index.htm

Map Sources: NCTA, *Rome to Finger Lakes Trail (NY-04)*

Road Walk to Next Segment: 8.2 miles (partially blazed)

Segment 7: Highland County Park, Morgan Hill State Forest, Labrador Hollow Nature Preserve

Range: Powerline southwest of West Lake Road (northwest of Deruyter Reservoir) to Cuyler Hill Rd (southeast of Cuyler). *(Note: This segment crosses some private land.)*

Total Trail Miles (Partially Certified): 25.9

Features: Tinker Falls and Spicer Falls

Partner Contact: Finger Lakes Trail Conference, www.fingerlakestrail.org

Local Information: Highland County Park (Highland County Forest) 315-683-5550

Map Sources:
NCTA, *Rome to Finger Lakes Trail (NY-04)*
FLTC, *M21 & O1**

Road Walk to Next Segment: 0.4 miles (blazed)

Segment 8: Cuyler Hill State Forest

Range: Cuyler Hill Road to Stoney Brook Road
Total Trail Miles: 0.3

Range: Stoney Brook Road to junction of Onondaga Branch and Finger Lakes Trail.
Total Trail Miles: 0.3

Partner Contact: Finger Lakes Trail Conference, www.fingerlakestrail.org

Map Sources:
  NCTA, *Rome to Finger Lakes Trail (NY-04)*
  FLTC, *M21**

Road Walk to Next Segment: 0.1 mile (blazed)

Segment 9: Cuyler Hill State Forest

Range: Junction of Onondaga Branch and Finger Lakes Trail to Solon Pond Road. *(Note: This segment crosses some private land.)*

Total Trail Miles (Partially Certified): 7.2

Partner Contact: Finger Lakes Trail Conference, www.fingerlakestrail.org

Map Sources: FLTC, *M21**

Segment 10: Taylor Valley State Forest

Range: Solon Pond Road to State Highway 41

Total Trail Miles (Certified): 9.2

Partner Contact: Finger Lakes Trail Conference, www.fingerlakestrail.org

Map Sources: FLTC, *M20 & M21**

Segment 11: Baker Schoolhouse – Hoxie Gorge State Forests

Range: State Highway 41 to Hoxie Gorge Road *(Note: This segment crosses some private land. A segment of this trail is closed by landowner during hunting season Oct. 1 – Dec. 31)*

Total Trail Miles (Certified): 8.9

Partner Contact: Finger Lakes Trail Conference, www.fingerlakestrail.org

Map Sources: FLTC, *M20 & M21**

Road Walk to Next Segment: 5.5 miles (blazed)

Tuller Hill State Forest
Photo by Eric Malmberg

Segment 12: Tuller Hill State Forest

Range: West River Road to Tone Road (south off of State Highway 392) *(Note: This segment crosses some private land.)*

Total Trail Miles (Partially Certified): 7.1

Partner Contact: Finger Lakes Trail Conference, www.fingerlakestrail.org

Map Sources: FLTC, *M19 & M20**

Segment 13: James D. Kennedy Memorial State Forest

(Note: These segments cross some private land.)

Range: Tone Road to O'Dell Road
Total Trail Miles (Partially Certified): 3.5
Road Walk to Next Segment: 0.3 mile (blazed)

Range: O'Dell Road to Daisy Hollow Road
Total Trail Miles (Partially Certified): 6.4
Road Walk to Next Segment: 5 miles (blazed)

Partner Contact: Finger Lakes Trail Conference, www.fingerlakestrail.org

Map Sources: FLTC, *M19**

Segment 14: Dryden Lake Area

(Note: These segments cross some private land.)

Range: Daisy Hollow Road to County Road 157
Total Trail Miles (Certified): 3.1
Road Walk to Next Segment: 0.3 mile (blazed)

Range: East Lake Road at railgrade southeast to East Lake Road at railgrade
Total Trail Miles (Certified): 0.6
Road Walk to Next Segment: 2 miles (blazed)

Partner Contact: Finger Lakes Trail Conference, www.fingerlakestrail.org

Map Sources: FLTC, *M19**

Segment 15: Hammond Hill & Robinson Hollow State Forests

Range: Star Stanton Hill Road to State Highway 79 (Note: This segment crosses some private land.)

Total Trail Miles: 6.5

Partner Contact: Finger Lakes Trail Conference, www.fingerlakestrail.org

Map Sources: FLTC, *M18**

Road Walk to Next Segment: 0.3 mile (blazed)

Segment 16: Potato Hill State Forest

(Note: These segments cross some private land.)

Range: State Highway 79 to Firetower Road
Total Trail Miles (Partially Certified): 1.2
Road Walk to Next Segment: 1 mile (blazed)

Range: Blackman Hill Road to Level Green Road
Total Trail Miles (Certified): 1.1
Road Walk to Next Segment: 0.2 mile (blazed)

Range: Level Green Road to Old Seventy Six Road
Total Trail Miles (Partially Certified): 1.9

Partner Contact: Finger Lakes Trail Conference, www.fingerlakestrail.org

Map Sources: FLTC, *M18**

Segment 17: Shindagin Hollow State Forest

(Note: These segments cross some private land.)

Range: Old Seventy Six Road to Shindagin Hollow Road
Total Trail Miles (Certified): 3.0
Road Walk to Next Segment: 0.1 mile (blazed)

Range: Shindagin Hollow Road to woods road east of Braley Hill Road
Total Trail Miles (Certified): 1.1
Road Walk to Next Segment: 0.5 mile (blazed)

Range: Braley Hill Road to Ridgeway Road
Total Trail Miles (Partially Certified): 2.9
Road Walk to Next Segment: 0.5 mile (blazed)

Partner Contact: Finger Lakes Trail Conference, www.fingerlakestrail.org

Map Sources: FLTC, *M18**

Segment 18: Danby State Forest

(Note: These segments cross some private land.)

Range: Eastman Hill Road to Eastman Hill Road
Total Trail Miles (Certified): 1.0
Road Walk to Next Segment: 2.5 miles (blazed)

Range: Durfee Hill Road to Comfort Road
Total Trail Miles (Certified): 8.1
Road Walk to Next Segment: 1.5 miles (blazed)

Partner Contact: Finger Lakes Trail Conference, www.fingerlakestrail.org

Map Sources: FLTC, *M17 & M18**

Segment 19: Jersey Hill Area

(Note: These segments cross private land.)

Range: Comfort Road to Layen Road
Total Trail Miles (Certified): 3.5
Road Walk to Next Segment: 1.3 miles (blazed)

Range: W. Jersey Hill Road to State Highway 13/34/96
Total Trail Miles (Certified): 2.8

Partner Contact: Finger Lakes Trail Conference, www.fingerlakestrail.org

Map Sources: FLTC, *M17**

Segment 20: Robert H. Treman State Park

(Note: These segments cross some private land.)

Range: State Highway 13/34/96 to Trumbull Road (2nd crossing)
Total Trail Miles (Partially Certified): 7.3
Road Walk to Next Segment: 0.6 mile (blazed)

Range: Rumsey Hill Road to Connecticut Hill Road
Total Trail Miles (Certified): 1.6
Road Walk to Next Segment: 1.1 miles (blazed)

Partner Contact: Finger Lakes Trail Conference, www.fingerlakestrail.org

Map Sources: FLTC, *M16**

Segment 21: Connecticut Hill Wildlife Management Area

(Note: These segments cross some private land.)

Range: Griffin Road to Cayutaville Road
Total Trail Miles (Certified): 0.7
Road Walk to Next Segment: 0.2 mile (blazed)

Range: Cayutaville Road to Tower Road
Total Trail Miles: 0.2 B
Road Walk to Next Segment: 0.2 mile (blazed)

Range: Tower Road to Gulf Road (just east of County Road 6)
Total Trail Miles (Certified): 8.8
Road Walk to Next Segment: 0.2 mile (blazed)

Partner Contact: Finger Lakes Trail Conference, www.fingerlakestrail.org

Map Sources: FLTC, *M16**

Segment 22: Cayuta Lake Area

Range: County Road 6 to State Road 228
Total Trail Miles (Certified): 1.0
Road Walk to Next Segment: 0.3 mile (blazed)

Range: West edge of housing area (northwest of State Highway 228) to Carley Road
Total Trail Miles (Certified): 1.8
Road Walk to Next Segment: 1.2 miles (blazed)

Partner Contact: Finger Lakes Trail Conference, www.fingerlakestrail.org

Map Sources: FLTC, *M15**

Segment 23: Texas Hollow State Forest

(Note: These segments cross some private land.)

Range: Steam Mill Road to Texas Hollow Road
Total Trail Miles (Partially Certified): 2.4
Road Walk to Next Segment: 0.2 miles (blazed)

Range: Texas Hollow Road to South Hill Road
Total Trail Miles (Partially Certified): 1.4
Road Walk to Next Segment: 1.0 mile (blazed)

Partner Contact: Finger Lakes Trail Conference, www.fingerlakestrail.org

Map Sources: FLTC, *M15**

Segment 24: Finger Lakes National Forest

Range: Burnt Hill Road to Satterly Hill Road *(Note: This segment crosses some private land. Trail between the twin tunnels and National Forest boundary, and from Satterly Hill Road west to the National Forest Boundary are closed by the landowner for hunting from Oct. 12 to Dec. 17 and May 1 to May 31. By-pass these sections of trail during the above dates using Satterly Hill Road.)*

Total Trail Miles (Partially Certified): 5.2

Features: The Forest encompasses 16,032 acres and has over 30 miles of inter-connecting trails that traverse gorges, ravines, pastures, and woodlands.

Partner Contact: Finger Lakes Trail Conference, www.fingerlakestrail.org

Local Information: Finger Lakes National Forest District Headquarters 607-546-4470, www.fs.fed.us/r9/gmfl/new_york/fingerlakes/

Map Sources: FLTC, *M15**

Road Walk to Next Segment: 3.0 miles (blazed)

Segment 25: Watkins Glen State Park

(Note: These segments cross some private land.)

Range: Middle Road to bridge over canal on State Highway 409/79
Total Trail Miles (Partially Certified): 2.4
Road Walk to Next Segment: 1.0 mile (blazed)

Range: State Highway 329 to VanZandt Hollow Road
Total Trail Miles (Partially Certified): 5.2

Partner Contact: Finger Lakes Trail Conference, www.fingerlakestrail.org

Map Sources: FLTC, *M14 & M15**

Segment 26: Sugar Hill & Goundry Hill State Forests

(Note: These segments cross some private land.)

Range: VanZandt Hollow Road to Goundry Hill Road
Total Trail Miles (Partially Certified): 13.4
Road Walk to Next Segment: 0.3 mile (blazed)

Range: Goundry Hill Road to County Road 17
Total Trail Miles (Partially Certified): 7.7
Road Walk to Next Segment: 2.0 miles (blazed)

Partner Contact: Finger Lakes Trail Conference, www.fingerlakestrail.org

Map Sources: FLTC, *M13 & M12**

Segment 27: Birdseye Hollow State Forest

Range: Sutryck Road to Longwell Road *(Note: This segment crosses some private land.)*

Total Trail Miles (Certified): 9.8

Partner Contact: Finger Lakes Trail Conference, www.fingerlakestrail.org

Map Sources: FLTC, *M12 & M13**

Road Walk to Next Segment: 1.2 miles (blazed)

Segment 28: Pleasant Valley

(Note: These segments cross some private land.)

Range: Longwell Road to Winding Stairs Road
Total Trail Miles (Certified): 1.4
Road Walk to Next Segment: 0.4 mile (blazed)

Range: Winding Stairs Road to State Highway 54
Total Trail Miles (Certified): 3.6
Road Walk to Next Segment: 0.5 mile (blazed)

Range: County Road 89 to Newton Road
Total Trail Miles (Certified): 4.1
Road Walk to Next Segment: 0.4 mile (blazed)

Range: Newton Road to Brewer Road
Total Trail Miles (Certified): 2.5
Road Walk to Next Segment: 0.3 mile (blazed)

Range: Barrett Road to Sandpit Road
Total Trail Miles (Certified): 3.1
Road Walk to Next Segment: 5.5 mile (blazed)

Partner Contact: Finger Lakes Trail Conference, www.fingerlakestrail.org

Map Sources: FLTC, *M12**

Segment 29: Robinson Hill & Snell Hill Area

(Note: These segments cross private land.)

Range: Sinclair Road to Harris Hill Road
Total Trail Miles (Certified): 3.9
Road Walk to Next Segment: 3.3 miles (blazed)

Range: Hughes Road to Burleson Road
Total Trail Miles (Certified): 1.8
Road Walk to Next Segment: 5.0 miles (blazed)

Partner Contact: Finger Lakes Trail Conference, www.fingerlakestrail.org

Map Sources: FLTC, *M10 & M11**

Segment 30: Burt Hill State Forest

Range: South Woods Road to Cunningham Creek Road *(Note: This segment crosses some private land.)*

Total Trail Miles (Certified): 2.8

Partner Contact: Finger Lakes Trail Conference, www.fingerlakestrail.org

Map Sources: FLTC, *M10**

Road Walk to Next Segment: 0.6 mile (blazed)

Segment 31: Hornell Area

(Note: These segments cross private land.)

Range: Cunningham Creek Road to Laine Road
Total Trail Miles (Certified): 0.5
Road Walk to Next Segment: 2.0 miles (blazed)

Range: Lower Glen Avenue to driveway of Econolodge motel off State Hwy 36
Total Trail Miles (Partially Certified): 4.5
Road Walk to Next Segment: 0.8 mile (blazed)

Range: Webbs Crossing Road (just west of State Road 65) to Webb Road
Total Trail Miles: 4.0
Road Walk to Next Segment: 3.0 miles (blazed)

Partner Contact: Finger Lakes Trail Conference, www.fingerlakestrail.org

Map Sources: FLTC, *M9 & M10**

Segment 32: Bully Hill State Forest

Range: Bishopville Road to Bush Road *(Note: This segment crosses some private land.)*

Total Trail Miles (Partially Certified): 6.8

Partner Contact: Finger Lakes Trail Conference, www.fingerlakestrail.org

Map Sources: FLTC, *M9**

Road Walk to Next Segment: 1.0 mile (blazed)

Segment 33: Klipnocky & Slader Creek State Forests

Range: Gas Springs Road to County Road 158 (Garwoods-Birdsall Road) *(Note: This segment crosses some private land.)*

Total Trail Miles (Partially Certified): 8.1

Partner Contact: Finger Lakes Trail Conference, www.fingerlakestrail.org

Map Sources: FLTC, *M9**

Road Walk to Next Segment: 0.7 mile (blazed)

Segment 34: Canaseraga Creek Area

Range: Isaman Hill Road to Mill Street *(Note: This segment crosses private land.)*

Total Trail Miles: 8.1

Partner Contact: Finger Lakes Trail Conference, www.fingerlakestrail.org

Map Sources: FLTC, *M8**

Road Walk to Next Segment: 1.7 miles (blazed)

Segment 35: Dalton & Hunt Area

(Note: These segments cross private land.)

Range: Old State Road (Country Road 24) to Cheese Factory Road
Total Trail Miles (Certified): 0.8
Road Walk to Next Segment: 0.2 mile (blazed)

Range: Hunt Hollow Road to Smith Hill Road
Total Trail Miles: 1.7
Road Walk to Next Segment: 0.3 mile (blazed)

Range: Smith Road to Pennycock Road
Total Trail Miles: 2.4
Road Walk to Next Segment: 0.1 mile (blazed)

Range: Pennycock Road to South River Road
Total Trail Miles: 0.7
Road Walk to Next Segment: 0.3 mile (blazed)

Range: South River Road to Hamton Road
Total Trail Miles: 1.7
Road Walk to Next Segment: 0.9 mile (blazed)

Partner Contact: Finger Lakes Trail Conference, www.fingerlakestrail.org

Map Sources: FLTC, *M7/L2 & M8**

Segment 36: Genesee Valley Greenway

Range: River Road near Whiskey Bridge (south of Portageville) to Tenefly Road
  (Note: This segment crosses private land.)

Total Trail Miles (Partially Certified): 4.3

Partner Contact: Finger Lakes Trail Conference, www.fingerlakestrail.org

Map Sources: FLTC, *M6 & M7/L2**

Road Walk to Next Segment: 1.8 miles (blazed)

Segment 37: Fillmore Area

(Note: These segments cross private land.)

Range: Graham Road to Pond Road
Total Trail Miles (Partially Certified): 3.8
Road Walk to Next Segment: 0.6 mile (blazed)

Range: Rice Road to State Highway 19
Total Trail Miles (Certified): 1.4
Road Walk to Next Segment: 0.6 mile (blazed)

Range: Buffalo Road to Ballard Road
Total Trail Miles (Certified): 4.7

Partner Contact: Finger Lakes Trail Conference, www.fingerlakestrail.org

Map Sources: FLTC, *M6**

Segment 38: Swift Hill State Forest

Range: Ballard Road to Rushford Road *(Note: This segment crosses some private land.)*

Total Trail Miles (Partially Certified): 3.3

Partner Contact: Finger Lakes Trail Conference, www.fingerlakestrail.org

Map Sources: FLTC, *M5 & M6**

Road Walk to Next Segment: 5.4 miles (blazed)

Segment 39: Farmersville State Forest

Range: Huyck Road to West Branch Road

Total Trail Miles (Certified): 2.7

Partner Contact: Finger Lakes Trail Conference, www.fingerlakestrail.org

Map Sources: FLTC, *M5**

Road Walk to Next Segment: 1.4 miles (blazed)

Segment 40: Bush Hill State Forest

Range: Stebbins Road to State Highway 98 *(Note: This segment crosses some private land.)*

Total Trail Miles (Partially Certified): 8.8

Partner Contact: Finger Lakes Trail Conference, www.fingerlakestrail.org

Map Sources: FLTC, *M5 & M4**

Road Walk to Next Segment: 2.0 miles (blazed)

Segment 41: Bear Creek State Forest

Range: Upper Bear Creek Road to Bear Creek Road

Total Trail Miles (Certified): 1.9

Partner Contact: Finger Lakes Trail Conference, www.fingerlakestrail.org

Map Sources: FLTC, *M4**

Road Walk to Next Segment: 2.0 miles (blazed)

Segment 42: Boyce Hill State Forest

(Note: These segments cross some private land.)

Range: Jackson Road to State Highway 242
Total Trail Miles (Partially Certified): 2.7
Road Walk to Next Segment: 2.0 miles (blazed)

Range: State Highway 242 to Fancy Tract Road
Total Trail Miles (Certified): 2.3
Road Walk to Next Segment: 0.5 mile (blazed)

Partner Contact: Finger Lakes Trail Conference, www.fingerlakestrail.org

Map Sources: FLTC, *M4**

Segment 43: Conservation Trail

(Note: These segments cross private land.)

Range: Fancy Tract Road to Fancy Tract Road
Total Trail Miles (Partially Certified): 1.9
Road Walk to Next Segment: 0.7 mile (blazed)

Range: Fancy Tract Road to Irish Hill Road
Total Trail Miles: 2.8
Road Walk to Next Segment: 0.2 mile (blazed)

Range: Irish Hill Road to Cotter Road
Total Trail Miles: 0.7
Road Walk to Next Segment: 0.6 mile (blazed)

Range: Cotter Road to Poverty Hill Road
Total Trail Miles: 2.6
Road Walk to Next Segment: 0.2 mile (blazed)

Range: Poverty Hill Road to Hencoop Hollow Road
Total Trail Miles: 3.5
Road Walk to Next Segment: 0.4 mile (blazed)

Partner Contact: Finger Lakes Trail Conference, www.fingerlakestrail.org

Map Sources: FLTC, *M3/CT3 & M4**

Rock City State Forest
Photo by Bill Menke

Segment 44: Conservation Trail – Rock City State Forest

Range: Dirt road south of State Highway 242 to Rock City Road *(Note: This segment crosses some private land.)*

Total Trail Miles (Partially Certified): 8.3

Partner Contact: Finger Lakes Trail Conference, www.fingerlakestrail.org

Map Sources: FLTC, *M3/CT3**

Road Walk to Next Segment: 1.5 miles (blazed)

Segment 45: Conservation Trail – Bucktooth State Forest

(Note: These segments cross some private land.)

Range: Wood Hollow Road to Fourth Street
Total Trail Miles: 2.4
Road Walk to Next Segment: 1.0 mile (blazed)

Range: East Branch Bucktooth Run Road to Sunfish Run Road
Total Trail Miles (Partially Certified): 7.7
Road Walk to Next Segment: 4.0 miles (blazed)

Partner Contact: Finger Lakes Trail Conference, www.fingerlakestrail.org

Map Sources: FLTC, *M2/CT2**

Segment 46: Conservation Trail – Allegany State Park

Range: Bay State Road to New York/Pennsylvania state line *(Note: This segment crosses some private land.)*

Total Trail Miles (Certified): 20.8

Features: The state park is the largest state park in New York State and the third largest state park in the country. It has many diverse facilities and is considered a (65,000 acre) nature preserve with acres of undisturbed woodland.

Partner Contact: Finger Lakes Trail Conference, www.fingerlakestrail.org

Local Information: Allegany State Park
www.allegheny-online.com/NYalleganypark.html

Map Sources: FLTC, *M1/CT1**

Additional Information

* To order maps from Finger Lakes Trail Conference, visit www.fingerlakestrail.org, or call 585-658-9320, a major credit card is needed. The maps can be purchased as a set or individually.

For more information regarding lodging, other types of accommodations, or other general tourism information about the state of New York, try www.iloveny.com/main.asp

Pennsylvania

Natural and cultural features are blended together along the trail as it crosses northwestern Pennsylvania. The trail enters the state along the Allegheny Reservoir and meanders southward through scenic rolling hills and stream valleys in the Allegheny National Forest. The route joins the Baker Trail, and follows it through state forest lands and Cook Forest State Park. From this park, interspersed with road walking in various places throughout the state, the trail route heads southwestward, paralleling portions of the Clarion and Allegheny Rivers. Through Butler County, the trail traverses state game lands in hilly and both forested and open segments. The Glacier Ridge segment in Moraine State Park reminds users of the origin of the surrounding landscape. In McConnells Mill State Park, the gorge of Slippery Rock Creek provides an unusually scenic setting for the trail, a 19th century covered bridge and a historic operating grist mill with its waterfalls. The trail has recently been completed through private and State Game Lands from the town of Wampum to the Ohio line.

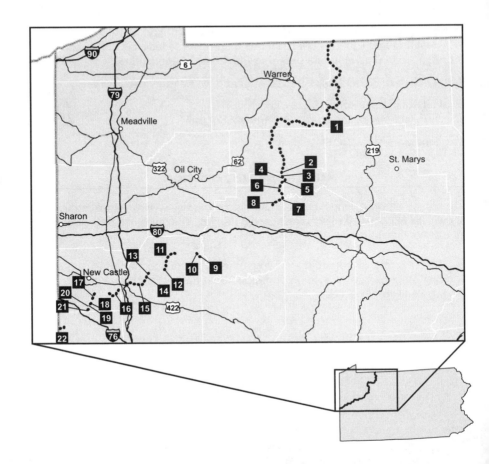

Allegheny National Forest
Photo by Rich Pfeiffer

Segment 1: Allegheny National Forest

Range: New York/Pennsylvania state line to Henrys Mills Road
Total Trail Miles (Certified): 51.3
Road Walk to Next Segment: 0.5 mile (blazed)

Range: State Road 666 at Henrys Mills to State Road 666 (north of Kellettville)
Total Trail Miles (Certified): 27.8
Road Walk to Next Segment: 2.3 miles (blazed)

Range: Forest Road 127 east of Kellettville to south forest boundary (west of Gifoyle)
Total Trail Miles (Certified): 14.0

Features: Scenic outcroppings, overlooks and beautiful views of Salmon Creek Valley.

Local Volunteer Group: Allegheny National Forest Chapter of NCTA
www.northcountrytrail.org/anf/index.htm

Local Information: Allegheny National Forest,
814-723-5150, www.fs.fed.us/r9/allegheny/

Map Sources:
NCTA, *Allegheny National Forest Segment (PA-01)*
NCTA, *Southern Allegheny National Forest & Cook Forest State Park (T203)*
NCTA, *Hutchins Guidebook - NCT in Pennsylvania (M201)*

Segment 2: State Game Lands 24

Range: Allegheny National Forest south boundary/State Game Lands 24 north boundary (west of Gifoyle) to State Game Lands 24 south boundary (east of Vowinckel)-majority follows Baker Trail

Total Trail Miles: 2.9

Features: Open field hiking amid beaver park

Partner Contacts: Hostelling International-USA, Pittsburgh Council http://trfn.clpgh.org/ayh

Local Information: State Game Lands 24, Northwest regional office 814-432-3187, www.pgc.state.pa.us/land/index.asp

Map Sources:
NCTA, *Hutchins Guidebook - NCT in Pennsylvania (M201)*
NCTA, *Southern Allegheny National Forest & Cook Forest State Park (T203)*
Hostelling Int'l - USA, Pittsburgh Council, *Baker Trail Guide*

Segment 3: Baker Trail

Range: State Game Lands 24 to Clear Creek State Forest *(Note: This segment crosses some private land.)*
Total Trail Miles: 1

Partner Contacts: Hostelling International-USA, Pittsburgh Council http://trfn.clpgh.org/ayh

Map Sources:
NCTA, *Hutchins Guidebook - NCT in Pennsylvania (M201)*
NCTA, *Southern Allegheny National Forest & Cook Forest State Park (T203)*
Hostelling Int'l - USA, Pittsburgh Council, *Baker Trail Guide*

Segment 4: Baker Trail - Clear Creek State Forest

Range: West boundary of Clear Creek State Forest to south boundary of Clear Creek State Forest
Total Trail Miles (Certified): 1.5

Features: Cross meandering Maple Creek on bridge and into a stand of pines.

Partner Contacts: Hostelling International-USA, Pittsburgh Council http://trfn.clpgh.org/ayh

Local Information: Clear Creek State Forest, 814-226-1901, www.dcnr.state.pa.us/forestry/stateforests/forests/clearcreek/clearcreek.htm

Map Sources:
NCTA, *Hutchins Guidebook - NCT in Pennsylvania (M201)*
NCTA, *Southern Allegheny National Forest & Cook Forest State Park (T203)*
Hostelling Int'l - USA, Pittsburgh Council, *Baker Trail Guide*

Segment 5: Baker Trail

Range: Clear Creek State Forest boundary to Jack Hollow Road to northeast boundary of Cook Forest State Park *(Note: This segment crosses some private land.)*

Total Trail Miles: 0.2

Features: Forest hiking

Partner Contact: Hostelling International-USA, Pittsburgh Council
http://trfn.clpgh.org/ayh

Map Sources:
NCTA, *Hutchins Guidebook - NCT in Pennsylvania (M201)*
NCTA, *Southern Allegheny National Forest & Cook Forest State Park (T203)*
Hostelling Int'l - USA, Pittsburgh Council, *Baker Trail Guide*

Road Walk to Next Segment: 0.5 mile (blazed)

Segment 6: Baker Trail – Cook Forest State Park

Range: Northeast boundary of Cook Forest State Park to southwest boundary of Cook Forest State Park

Total Trail Miles (Certified): 8.9

Features: Cook Forest State Park has an awesome stand of virgin forest, an expansive view of the Clarion River from Seneca Point near the fire tower and a short hike alongside the Clarion River.

Partner Contact: Hostelling International-USA, Pittsburgh Council
http://trfn.clpgh.org/ayh

Local Information: Cook Forest State Park, 814-744-8407,
www.dcnr.state.pa.us/stateparks/parks/cookforest.asp

Map Sources:
NCTA, *Hutchins Guidebook - NCT in Pennsylvania (M201)*
NCTA, *Southern Allegheny National Forest & Cook Forest State Park (T203)*
Hostelling Int'l - USA, Pittsburgh Council, *Baker Trail Guide*

Segment 7: Clarion River

Range: Southwestern boundary of Cook Forest State Park to Highland Road
(Note: This segment crosses some private land.)

Total Trail Miles: 0.7

Partner Contact: Hostelling International-USA, Pittsburgh Council
http://trfn.clpgh.org/ayh

Map Sources:
NCTA, *Hutchins Guidebook - NCT in Pennsylvania (M201)*
NCTA, *Southern Allegheny National Forest & Cook Forest State Park (T203)*

Road Walk to Next Segment: 0.5 mile (blazed)

Segment 8: State Game Lands 283

Range: Gravel Lick Road to dirt road south off of Miolia Road between Helen
Furnace and Scotch Hill

Total Trail Miles: 4.1

Features: Forest hiking in hilly terrain

Local Volunteer Group: Clarion Chapter of NCTA
www.northcountrytrail.org/cla/index.htm

Local Information: State Game Lands 283, Northwest regional office
814-432-3187, www.pgc.state.pa.us/land/index.asp

Map Sources:
NCTA, *Hutchins Guidebook - NCT in Pennsylvania (M201)*
NCTA, *Southern Allegheny National Forest & Cook Forest State Park (T203)*

Road Walk to Next Segment: 35 miles (blazed)

Segment 9: Bear Creek

Range: Jackson Avenue (south of Parker) to east boundary of State Game Land
95 (southwest of Parker) *(Note: This segment crosses some private land.)*

Total Trail Miles: 0.1

Features: Hiking on old railroad bed

Local Volunteer Group: Clarion Chapter of NCTA
www.northcountrytrail.org/cla/index.htm

Segment 10: State Game Lands 95

Range: East boundary of State Game Lands 95 (southwest of Parker) to northwest boundary of State Game Lands 95 at E. Eldorado Road

Total Trail Miles: 2.6

Features: Views of Bear Creek, hilly forest hiking, stream crossings on excellent bridges, enjoyable hemlock lined valleys and remnants of yesteryear's oil production.

Local Volunteer Group: Butler Chapter of NCTA
www.northcountrytrail.org/but/index.htm

Local Information: State Game Lands 95, Northwest regional office
814-432-3187, www.pgc.state.pa.us/land/index.asp

Road Walk to Next Segment: 8.0 miles (not blazed)

Segment 11: State Game Lands 95

Range: Southeast boundary of State Game Lands 95 at Leonard Road (west of Argentine) to southwest boundary of State Game Lands 95 (southeast of Five Points)

Total Trail Miles: 9.6

Features: Open valley and hill hiking, views of lakes and forest

Local Volunteer Group:
Butler Chapter of NCTA - www.northcountrytrail.org/but/index.htm
Rock Chapter of NCTA - www.northcountrytrail.org/rok/index.htm

Local Information: State Game Lands 95, Northwest regional office
814-432-3187, www.pgc.state.pa.us/land/index.asp

Segment 12: Northwest Sanitary Landfill

Range: Southwest boundary of State Game Lands 95 (southeast of Five Points) to State Road 308 (south of Five Points) *(Note: This segment crosses some private land.)*

Total Trail Miles: 1.1

Features: Forest hiking

Local Volunteer Group: Rock Chapter of NCTA
www.northcountrytrail.org/rok/index.htm

Road Walk to Next Segment: 6.5 miles (not blazed)

Segment 13: Old Stone House Historic Site

Range: Driveway to Old Stone House off Halston Road to State Road 8 (southeast of Slippery Rock)

Total Trail Miles: 0.6

Features: Historic Stone House, formerly a stage coach inn

Local Volunteer Group: Rock Chapter of NCTA
www.northcountrytrail.org/rok/index.htm

Map Sources: NCTA, *McConnells Mill & Moraine State Parks (T201)*

Segment 14: Jennings Environmental Education Center

Range: State Road 8 to Moraine State Park

Total Trail Miles (Certified): 0.9

Features: Jennings Environmental Education Center featuring a prairie with rare Blazing Star flowers in August and even rarer massasauga rattle snakes, old one room school house being renovated, forest vale hiking along a lazy clear stream and modern nature center.

Local Volunteer Group: Greater Pittsburgh Chapter of NCTA
www.northcountrytrail.org/gpt/index.htm

Local Information: Jennings Environmental Education Center, 724-794-6011

Map Sources:
NCTA, *McConnells Mill & Moraine State Parks (T201)*
NCTA, *Hutchins Guidebook - NCT in Pennsylvania (M201)*

Jennings Environmental Education Center
Photo by Bill Menke

Segment 15: Moraine State Park

Range: Jennings Environmental Learning Center to North Shore Drive in Mc-Danels area of Moraine State Park

Total Trail Miles (Certified): 13.6

Features: Hilly forest hiking with a great view of Lake Arthur, a short walk along Lake Arthur's Trout Cove, a side trail to the Davis Hollow Outdoors Center and a walk around a large peaceful pond.

Local Volunteer Group:
Greater Pittsburgh Chapter of NCTA - www.northcountrytrail.org/gpt/index.htm
Butler Chapter of NCTA - www.northcountrytrail.org/but/index.htm

Local Information: Moraine State Park
724-368-8811, www.dcnr.state.pa.us/stateparks/parks/moraine.asp

Map Sources:
NCTA, *McConnells Mill & Moraine State Parks (T201)*
NCTA, *Hutchins Guidebook - NCT in Pennsylvania (M201)*

Road Walk to Next Segment: 2.6 miles (blazed)

Segment 16: McConnells Mill State Park

Range: Alpha Pass near McConnells Mill Road in McConnells Mill State Park to Hells Hollow Trailhead at Shaffer Road

Total Trail Miles (Certified): 7.6

Features: Incredible area with huge rocks, great views of geologically significant Slippery Rock Creek, an operating grist mill, a covered bridge, deep hemlock lined valleys and hilly forest hiking.

Local Volunteer Group: Wampum Chapter of NCTA
www.northcountrytrail.org/wam/index.htm

Local Information: McConnells Mill State Park, 724-368-8811,
www.dcnr.state.pa.us/stateparks/parks/mcconnellsmill.asp

Map Sources:
NCTA, *McConnells Mill & Moraine State Parks (T201)*
NCTA, *Hutchins Guidebook - NCT in Pennsylvania (M201)*

Road Walk to Next Segment: 4.6 miles (not blazed)

McConnells Mill
Photo by Bill Menke

Segment 17: CEMEX North

Range: Snake Run Road (Northeast of Wampum) to River Road *(Note: This segment crosses some private land.)*

Total Trail Miles: 4.6

Local Volunteer Group: Wampum Chapter of NCTA
www.northcountrytrail.org/wam/index.htm

Road Walk to Next Segment: 0.6 miles (not blazed)

Segment 18: Wampum Borough

Range: Junction of River Road and State Road 288 to State Road 18 (along city streets) *(Note: This segment crosses some private land.)*

Total Trail Miles (Certified): 0.3

Local Volunteer Group: Wampum Chapter of NCTA
www.northcountrytrail.org/wam/index.htm

Road Walk to Next Segment: 0.7 miles (not blazed)

Segment 19: Gateway Property

Range: State Road 18 to Cemex Property at two track *(Note: This segment crosses some private land.)*

Total Trail Miles: 0.8

Local Volunteer Group: Wampum Chapter of NCTA
www.northcountrytrail.org/wam/index.htm

Segment 20: CEMEX Property

Range: Gateway property at two track to State Game Lands 148 *(Note: This segment crosses some private land.)*

Total Trail Miles: 0.5

Local Volunteer Group: Wampum Chapter of NCTA
www.northcountrytrail.org/wam/index.htm

Segment 21: State Game Lands 148

Range: Northeast corner of State Game Lands 148 to Wampum-New Galilee Road just north of the Lawrence/Beaver county line

Total Trail Miles: 2.1

Local Volunteer Group: Wampum Chapter of NCTA
www.northcountrytrail.org/wam/index.htm

Local Information: State Game Lands 148, Southwest regional office, 724-238-9523, www.pgc.state.pa.us/land/index.asp

Road Walk to Next Segment: 10 miles (not blazed)

Segment 22: State Game Lands 285

Range: Watts Mill Road southwest of Cannelton to State Road 251/154 at the Ohio state line

Total Trail Miles (Certified): 3.8

Local Volunteer Group: Wampum Chapter of NCTA
www.northcountrytrail.org/wam/index.htm

Local Information: State Game Lands 285, Southwest regional office, 724-238-9523, www.pgc.state.pa.us/land/index.asp

Additional Information

For more information regarding lodging, other types of accommodations, or other general tourism information about the state of Pennsylvania, try www.state.pa.us

Ohio

The North Country Trail makes a U-shaped sweep through Ohio. For much of the route, it follows the Buckeye Trail. In eastern Ohio, the trail heads westward toward the historic communal settlement of Zoar paralleling Sandy Creek and Little Beaver Creek, a national scenic river. Continuing south, it links a series of reservoirs and recreation areas, eventually reaching the Wayne National Forest. The trail follows the scenic Little Muskingham River through the forest and exits near Marietta. The trail route crosses long stretches of private lands to the outskirts of Cincinnati. Along the way are the rock bluffs and caves of the scenic Hocking Hill region and State memorials commemorating prehistoric Indian cultures. Near Cincinnati, the North Country Trail joins a rail-trail that continues north to Springfield. Developed and maintained by a combination of state, county and municipal agencies, the trail parallels the Little Miami National Scenic River. At Springfield, the trail route skirts northward around Dayton while the Buckeye Trail continues as an alternate route through the city. In western Ohio, the trail follows the remnants of the Old Miami and Erie Canal.

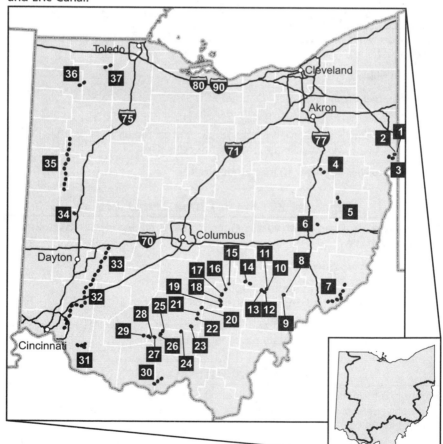

Segment 1: Beaver Creek State Forest

Range: Railgrade at Jackson Road to Pancake-Clarkson Road

Total Trail Miles: 1.2

Local Volunteer Group: Great Trail Sandy Beaver Canal Chapter of NCTA, www.northcountrytrail.org/gts/index.htm

Local Information: Beaver Creek State Forest, 330-339-2205 www.dnr.state.oh.us/forestry/Forests/stateforests/beavercreek.htm

Road Walk to Next Segment: 0.3 miles (not blazed)

Segment 2: Sheepskin Hollow State Nature Preserve

Range: Pancake-Clarkson Road to State Highway 170 (Note: This segment crosses some private land).

Total Trail Miles: 3.2

Local Volunteer Group: Great Trail Sandy Beaver Canal Chapter of NCTA, www.northcountrytrail.org/gts/index.htm

Local Information: Sheepskin Hollow State Nature Preserve www.dnr.state.oh.us/dnap/location/sheepskin.htm

Road Walk to Next Segment: 7.4 miles (not blazed)

Segment 3: Beaver Creek State Park

Range: Sprucevale to Family Camp Area

Total Trail Miles (Certified): 6.3

Features: The Park is comprised of various habitats including bottomlands, a gorge, forest and Little Beaver Creek, a national and state wild and scenic river. The remnants of the Sandy and Beaver Canal and lock, a spur of the Ohio-Erie Canal, are found throughout the park. A pioneer village and water powered grist mill as well as a restored lock are available for viewing.

Local Volunteer Group: Great Trail Sandy Beaver Canal Chapter of NCTA www.northcountrytrail.org/gts/index.htm

Local Information: Beaver Creek State Park, 330-385-3091, www.dnr.state.oh.us/parks/parks/beaverck.htm

Road Walk to Next Segment: 60 miles (not blazed)

Segment 4: Buckeye Trail

Range: Tuscarawas County Road 82 (south of Zoar) to County Road 109 (north of Somerdale)

Total Trail Miles (Certified): 5.7

Features: The Zoar historical communal settlement is located off the trail about .5 miles from this certified segment. Many of the German-style structures built by the Zoarites have been restored and are open to the public as Zoar Village State Memorial.

Partner Contact: Buckeye Trail Association, www.buckeyetrail.org

Map Sources: BTA, *Massilon Section**

Road Walk to Next Segment: 17.3 miles (blazed)

Segment 5: Muskingum Watershed Conservation District

Range: Deer Road (T-116) at Entrance to Clows Marina on Leesville Lake to Autumn Road
Total Trail Miles (Not Certified): 1.5
Road Walk to Next Segment: 7.4 miles (blazed)

Range: Township Road 213 along Tappan Reservoir to McGonigal Road along Tappan Reservoir
Total Trail Miles (Certified): 6.6
Road Walk to Next Segment: 0.2 mile (blazed)

Range: McGonigal Road (just North of Moravian Trail Road) to Moravian Trail Road along Tappan Reservoir
Total Trail Miles (Certified): 0.8
Road Walk to Next Segment: 3.5 miles (blazed)

Range: Long Road at Clendening Lake Road (State Highway 799) to State Road 799 at North end southern causeway on Clendening Reservoir.
Total Trail Miles (Certified): 9.9
Road Walk to Next Segment: 6.0 miles (blazed)

Range: US Highway 22 west of Piedmont to Thin Road
Total Trail Miles (Certified): 5.2
Road Walk to Next Segment: 19.7 miles (blazed)

Partner Contact: Buckeye Trail Association, www.buckeyetrail.org

Map Sources: BTA, *Bowerston Section**

Segment 6: Salt Fork Wildlife Area

Range: NR-55 to Campground on NR-59 (west of Parker Road/T-587)

Total Trail Miles (Certified): 3.2

Features: The Salt Fork Wildlife Area is adjacent to eastern Ohio's Salt Fork State Park and the environment is 1/3 mature woods, 1/3 grasslands and 1/3 is home to a variety of small trees and shrubs. The wilderness area offers an abundance of wood ducks, wading birds and shore birds at the 80-acre marsh on the eastern end of the area and along the Salt Fork Lake's 74 miles of shoreline. Visitors frequently report bald eagle sightings near the park's lakes and waterways.

Partner Contact: Buckeye Trail Association, www.buckeyetrail.org

Local Information: Salt Fork Wildlife Area, 740-489-5021

Map Sources: BTA, *Belle Valley Section**

Road Walk to Next Segment: 65 miles (partially blazed)

Segment 7: Wayne National Forest

Range: Poulton to Monroe/Washington County Line
Total Trail Miles (Certified): 5.2
Features: The terrain is hilly in the National Forest. Deer, grouse and turkeys can be seen as well as being a great place to look at fall colors.
Road Walk to Next Segment: 2.5 miles (not blazed)

Range: County Road 138 (northwest of Glass) to State Road 26 (northeast of Hills)
Total Trail Miles (Certified): 31.3
Features: This part of the National Forest is a mix of open land and forest and provides a wide variety of wildlife habitats.
Road Walk to Next Segment: 25 miles (not blazed)

Partner Contact: Buckeye Trail Association, www.buckeyetrail.org

Local Information: Wayne National Forest (Marietta Unit) 740-373-9055, www.fs.fed.us/r9/wayne/

Map Sources:
NCTA, *Hutchins Guidebook - NCT Through Ohio's Wayne N.F. (M301)*

Segment 8: Buckeye Trail

Range: Iron gate on Township Road 23 (Southwest of State Hwy 792, southwest of Stockport) to improved section of Township Road 23 (east of Todds)

Total Trail Miles (Certified): 1.1

Partner Contact: Buckeye Trail Association, www.buckeyetrail.org

Map Sources: BTA, *Stockport Section**

Road Walk to Next Segment: 1.5 miles (blazed)

Segment 9: Buckeye Trail

Range: Junction of County Road 66 and driveway to State Road 377 (north of Chesterhill)

Total Trail Miles (Certified): 2.4

Partner Contact: Buckeye Trail Association, www.buckeyetrail.org

Map Sources: BTA, *Stockport Section**

Road Walk to Next Segment: 17 miles (blazed)

Segment 10: Wayne National Forest

Range: County Road 58 to County Road 15 (between Ringgold and Vicksville)

Total Trail Miles (Certified): 1.0

Features: Heron, loon, osprey, beaver and otter are examples of the variety of wildlife can be seen primarily along the waterway in this section of the National Forest. In the upland forests area, commonly seen mammals are white-tailed deer, gray fox, woodchuck, opossum, and gray squirrel. Birds such as turkey, ruffed grouse, pileated woodpecker and wood duck can also be viewed.

Partner Contact: Buckeye Trail Association, www.buckeyetrail.org

Local Information:
Wayne National Forest (Supervisor's Office and Athens Ranger District) 740-753-0101, www.fs.fed.us/r9/wayne/

Map Sources: BTA, *New Straitsville Section**

Road Walk to Next Segment: 1.0 miles (blazed)

Segment 11: Burr Oak State Park

Range: C-15 to Tom Jenkins Dam

Total Trail Miles (Partially Certified): 12.5

Features: Burr Oak State Park includes miles of forested ridges and hollows that comprise the foothills of the Appalachian Mountains. The woodlands support a variety of wildlife including white-tailed deer, ruffed grouse, box turtles and the elusive wild turkey. The forest is comprised of numerous hardwoods but is dominated by stately oaks and hickories. In autumn, the forest displays spectacular fall colors as leaves turn to deep reds, brilliant yellows and burnt oranges. Woodland wildflowers are equally as impressive in the spring when violets, Dutchman's breeches, trillium, rare orchids, bloodroot and hepatica are in bloom. The lake's shore is inhabited by the industrious beaver and various waterfowl species.

Partner Contact: Buckeye Trail Association, www.buckeyetrail.org

Local Information: Burr Oak State Park,
740-767-3570, www.dnr.state.oh.us/parks/parks/burroak.htm

Map Sources:
BTA, *New Straitsville Section**
NCTA, *Hutchins Guidebook - From Burr Oak State Park to Milford (M3032)*

Segment 12: Buckeye Trail

Range: Tom Jenkins Dam to State Road 13 (south of Burr Oak)

Total Trail Miles (Certified): 0.4

Partner Contact: Buckeye Trail Association, www.buckeyetrail.org

Map Sources:
BTA, *New Straitsville Section #30**
NCTA, *Hutchins Guidebook - From Burr Oak State Park to Milford (M3032)*

Wayne National Forest
Photo by Bill Menke

Segment 13: Wayne National Forest

Range: State Road 13 (south of Burr Oak) to forest boundary near Antle Orchard Road (east of McLeish)

Total Trail Miles (Certified): 3.0

Features: There are a variety of hardwoods; predominately oak and hickory in this section of the National Forest.

Partner Contact: Buckeye Trail Association, www.buckeyetrail.org

Local Information: Wayne National Forest (Supervisor's Office & Athens Ranger District), 740-753-0101, www.fs.fed.us/r9/wayne/

Map Sources:
BTA, *New Straitsville Section**
NCTA, *Hutchins Guidebook - From Burr Oak State Park to Milford (M3032)*

Road Walk to Next Segment: 11.5 miles (blazed)

Segment 14: Wayne National Forest

Range: Salem Road (southeast of New Straitsville) to Township Road 190

Total Trail Miles (Certified): 15.8

Features: The Wayne National Forest in this segment is comprised of rolling Appalachian foothills, with rock shelters, bluffs, and coves that are home to many rare plants.

Partner Contact: Buckeye Trail Association, www.buckeyetrail.org

Local Information: Wayne National Forest (Supervisor's Office & Athens Ranger District), 740-753-0101, www.fs.fed.us/r9/wayne/

Map Sources:
BTA, *New Straitsville Section**
NCTA, *Hutchins Guidebook - From Burr Oak State Park to Milford (M3032)*

Road Walk to Next Segment: 12 miles (blazed)

Segment 15: Buckeye Trail

Range: West end of Township Road 44 (Walnut-Dowler Road) to beginning of maintenance of Helber Road

Total Trail Miles (Certified): 1.9

Partner Contact: Buckeye Trail Association, www.buckeyetrail.org

Map Sources:
BTA, *Old Mans Cave Section**
NCTA, *Hutchins Guidebook - From Burr Oak State Park to Milford (M3032)*

Road Walk to Next Segment: 5.0 miles (blazed)

Segment 16: Buckeye Trail

Range: Lake Logan Road to Murphy Road (all is west of Lake Logan State Park and south of Enterprise)

Total Trail Miles (Certified): 1.2

Partner Contact: Buckeye Trail Association, www.buckeyetrail.org

Map Sources:
BTA, *Old Mans Cave Section #32**
NCTA, *Hutchins Guidebook - From Burr Oak State Park to Milford (M3032)*

Road Walk to Next Segment: 6.0 miles (blazed)

Segment 17: Hocking State Forest

Range: Rocky Fork Road to Kreashbaum Road

Total Trail Miles (Certified): 2.6

Features: This area of the trail is managed for timber and wildlife habitat. Ninety-nine acres of forest land has been set aside for rock climbing and rappelling.

Partner Contact: Buckeye Trail Association, www.buckeyetrail.org

Local Information: Hocking State Forest, 740-385-4402, www.dnr.state.oh.us/forestry/Forests/stateforests/hocking.htm

Map Sources:
BTA, *Old Mans Cave Section**
NCTA, *Hutchins Guidebook - From Burr Oak State Park to Milford (M3032)*

Road Walk to Next Segment: 2.0 miles (blazed)

Segment 18: Hocking State Forest

Range: Big Pine Road to Culp Road north of Cedar Grove *(Note: This segment crosses some private land.)*

Total Trail Miles (Certified): 2.6

Features: An area has been set aside for rock climbing and rappelling. Plant species commonly found farther north mix with typically southern species to provide an unusual variety of native plant life and associated wildlife

Partner Contact: Buckeye Trail Association, www.buckeyetrail.org

Local Information: Hocking State Forest, 740-385-4402, www.dnr.state.oh.us/forestry/Forests/stateforests/hocking.htm

Map Sources:
BTA, *Old Mans Cave Section**
NCTA, *Hutchins Guidebook - From Burr Oak State Park to Milford (M3032)*

Road Walk to Next Segment: 0.6 mile (blazed)

Buckeye Trail
Photo by Dick Bolton

Segment 19: Hocking Hills State Park

Range: State Road 664 to Ash Cave parking area at State Road 56

Total Trail Miles (Certified): 6.0

Features: This segment of the trail contains many waterfalls, gorges, and caves. There is a huge tree diversity including hemlocks. This area is the true foothills of the Appalachians and the park is at the point where the glacier stopped. There are a number of rare and endangered species, including some that grow on cliff walls.

Partner Contact: Buckeye Trail Association, www.buckeyetrail.org

Local Information: Hocking Hill State Park, 740-385-6841, www.dnr.state.oh.us/parks/parks/hocking.htm

Map Sources:
BTA, *Old Mans Cave Section**
NCTA, *Hutchins Guidebook - From Burr Oak State Park to Milford (M3032)*

Road Walk to Next Segment: 18 miles (blazed)

Segment 20: Tar Hollow State Forest

Range: Clark Hollow Road at Ranger Station (west of State Hwy 327) to South Ridge Road (near Piney Creek Road)

Total Trail Miles (Certified): 7.3

Features: A 16,000 acre forest with rolling hills and mostly oak trees on ridges. Deer and turkeys are the majority of wildlife in this area. A segment of the trail leads to a lake and another to a fire tower.

Partner Contact: Buckeye Trail Association, www.buckeyetrail.org

Local Information: Scioto Trail and Tar Hollow State Forests, 740-663-2538
www.dnr.state.oh.us/forestry/forests/stateforests/tarhollow.htm
www.dnr.state.oh.us/forestry/forests/stateforests/sciototrail.htm

Tar Hollow State Park, 740-887-4818,
www.dnr.state.oh.us/parks/parks/tarhollow.htm

Map Sources:
BTA, *Scioto Trail Section**
NCTA, *Hutchins Guidebook - From Burr Oak State Park to Milford (M3032)*

Road Walk to Next Segment: 2.0 miles (blazed)

Segment 21: Tar Hollow State Forest & Meade Corporation

Range: Junction of Sugar Run Road and South Ridge Road to north end of Bluelick Road *(Note: This segment crosses some private land.)*

Total Trail Miles (Certified): 2.4

Features: This area of the trail is composed of deep ravines and dense woodlands. The Fall pagent of colors is spectacular.

Partner Contact: Buckeye Trail Association, www.buckeyetrail.org

Local Information: Scioto Trail and Tar Hollow State Forests, 740-663-2538
www.dnr.state.oh.us/forestry/forests/stateforests/tarhollow.htm
www.dnr.state.oh.us/forestry/forests/stateforests/sciototrail.htm

Map Sources:
BTA, *Scioto Trail Section**
NCTA, *Hutchins Guidebook - From Burr Oak State Park to Milford (M3032)*

Road Walk to Next Segment: 1.0 miles (blazed)

Segment 22: Buckeye Trail

Range: Blue Lick Road to Buffalo Trails Campground (north of US Hwy 50) (all is northwest of Londonderry) *(Note: This segment crosses private land.)*

Total Trail Miles (Certified): 1.5

Partner Contact: Buckeye Trail Association, www.buckeyetrail.org

Map Sources:
BTA, *Scioto Trail Section**
NCTA, *Hutchins Guidebook - From Burr Oak State Park to Milford (M3032)*

Road Walk to Next Segment: 10 miles (blazed)

Segment 23: Buckeye Trail – Scioto Trail State Forest

Range: Higby Road (at Three Lock Road, north of Higby) to South Ridge Road

Total Trail Miles (Certified): 1.9

Features: The State Forest is composed of sandstone hills that are covered with a rich diverse forest. It is a stronghold for many exciting species of wildlife such as the timber rattlesnake and five-lined skink.

Partner Contact: Buckeye Trail Association, www.buckeyetrail.org

Local Information: Scioto Trail and Tar Hollow State Forests, 740-663-2538
www.dnr.state.oh.us/forestry/forests/stateforests/tarhollow.htm
www.dnr.state.oh.us/forestry/forests/stateforests/sciototrail.htm

Map Sources:
BTA, *Scioto Trail Section #34**
NCTA, *Hutchins Guidebook - From Burr Oak State Park to Milford (M3032)*

Road Walk to Next Segment: 8.5 miles (blazed)

Segment 24: Buckeye Trail

Range: Woods Hollow Road (southeast of Alma) to Prussia Road (northwest of Waverly)

Total Trail Miles (Certified): 2.5

Partner Contact: Buckeye Trail Association, www.buckeyetrail.org

Map Sources:
BTA, *Scioto Trail Section**
NCTA, *Hutchins Guidebook - From Burr Oak State Park to Milford (M3032)*

Road Walk to Next Segment: 12.3 miles (blazed)

Segment 25: Pike State Forest & Pike Lake State Park

Range: Morgans Fork Road (southwest of Nipgen) to Pike Lake Road
Total Trail Miles (Certified): 8.0
Road Walk to Next Segment: 0.5 mile (blazed)

Range: Pike Lane Road to Greenbriar Road at Auerville Road
Total Trail Miles (Certified): 3.1
Road Walk to Next Segment: 1.1 miles (blazed)

Range: Fire Tower Road (west of Morgantown) to Shoemaker Road (northwest of Latham)
Total Trail Miles (Certified): 3.4
Road Walk to Next Segment: 1.6 miles (blazed)

Features: Hilly terrain with dense forests that are a mix of hardwoods comprise the Pike State Forest. Wildflowers are diverse and create spectacular displays-spring through autumn. Several outcroppings of sandstone bedrock have been exposed in the forest. A variety wildlife can be seen at the ponds and open areas.

Partner Contact: Buckeye Trail Association, www.buckeyetrail.org

Local Information: Pike State Forest, 740-493-2441
www.dnr.state.oh.us/forestry/forests/stateforests/pike.htm

Pike Lake State Park, 740-493-2212
www.dnr.state.oh.us/parks/parks/pikelake.htm

Map Sources:
BTA, *Scioto Trail Section & Sinking Spring Section**
NCTA, *Hutchins Guidebook - From Burr Oak State Park to Milford (M3032)*

Segment 26: Latham Hatchery & Pike State Forest

Range: Laperall Road (west of Latham) to Bell Hollow Road (northwest of Cedar Fork) *(Note: This segment crosses some private land.)*

Total Trail Miles (Certified): 0.3

Partner Contact: Buckeye Trail Association, www.buckeyetrail.org

Local Information: Pike State Forest, 740-493-2441,
www.dnr.state.oh.us/forestry/forests/stateforests/pike.htm

Map Sources:
BTA, *Sinking Spring Section**
NCTA, *Hutchins Guidebook - From Burr Oak State Park to Milford (M3032)*

Road Walk to Next Segment: 1.6 miles (blazed)

Segment 27: Buckeye Trail

Range: Bell Hollow Road to Pike State Forest *(Note: This segment crosses some private land.)*

Total Trail Miles (Certified): 0.3

Partner Contact: Buckeye Trail Association, www.buckeyetrail.org

Map Sources:
BTA, *Sinking Spring Section**
NCTA, *Hutchins Guidebook - From Burr Oak State Park to Milford (M3032)*

Segment 28: Pike State Forest

Range: Pike State Forest to Fort Hill State Memorial

Total Trail Miles (Certified): 2.9

Features: The State Forest marks the boundary between the hilly eastern section and the flatter western portions of Ohio. The landscape of the Forest is characterized by dense forests of oak, hickory, tulip ash and other hardwoods. The forest and remote location of Pike Lake make an excellent habitat for forest animals.

Partner Contact: Buckeye Trail Association, www.buckeyetrail.org

Local Information: Pike State Forest, 740-493-2441

Map Sources:
BTA, *Sinking Spring Section**
NCTA, *Hutchins Guidebook - From Burr Oak State Park to Milford (M3032)*

Segment 29: Fort Hill State Memorial

Range: Fort Hill State Memorial (north of Sinking Spring)

Total Trail Miles (Certified): 4.9

Features: This hilly terrain contains an impressive diversity of bedrock, soils, flora and fauna. In the 1,200 acre preserve, there are three contiguous hiking trails. There is a small museum and one of the best preserved Indian hilltop enclosures in North America.

Partner Contact: Buckeye Trail Association, www.buckeyetrail.org

Local Information: Fort Hill State Memorial (Ohio Historical Society) 937-588-3221, 800-283-8905, www.ohiohistory.org/places/fthill/

Map Sources:
BTA, *Sinking Spring Section**
NCTA, *Hutchins Guidebook - From Burr Oak State Park to Milford (M3032)*

Road Walk to Next Segment: 49 miles (blazed)

Segment 30: Shawnee State Park & Forest

Range: Northernmost point of Main Trail to Sunshine Ridge Road

Total Trail Miles (Certified): 16.0

Features: The rugged beauty of this area has earned it the nickname "Little Smokies." There are wooded hills, abundant wildflowers and erosion-carved valleys. Three miles of the trail are located in the only Wilderness Area in Ohio. Forest wildlife includes white-tail deer, wild turkey, raccoon and various songbirds.

Partner Contact: Buckeye Trail Association, www.buckeyetrail.org

Local Information: Shawnee State Park, 740-858-6652, www.dnr.state.oh.us/parks/parks/shawnee.htm

Shawnee State Forest, 740-858-6685, www.dnr.state.oh.us/forestry/forests/stateforests/shawnee.htm

Map Sources:
BTA, *Shawnee Section**
NCTA, *Hutchins Guidebook - From Burr Oak State Park to Milford (M3032)*

Road Walk to Next Segment: 72.5 miles (blazed)

Segment 31: East Fork State Park

Range: Ridge Road to Slade Road
Total Trail Miles (Certified): 22.1
Road Walk to Next Segment: 2.0 miles (blazed)

Range: End of Slade Road to County Road 44
Total Trail Miles (Certified): 0.6
Road Walk to Next Segment: 18 miles (blazed)

Features: The landscape in the park is very diverse and scenic; and includes rugged hills, rocky cascades, abandoned farmland, marshy grasslands, open meadows and swamp forests. The heavily wooded forests are composed of maple, hickory, beech oak and cherry. Animals include deer, raccoons, skunks, squirrels, and Canadian geese.

Partner Contact: Buckeye Trail Association, www.buckeyetrail.org

Local Information: East Fork State Park, 513-734-4323, www.dnr.state.oh.us/parks/parks/eastfork.htm

Map Sources:
BTA, *Williamsburg Section**
NCTA, *Hutchins Guidebook - From Burr Oak State Park to Milford (M3032)*

Segment 32: Little Miami State Park

Range: Kroger Hills State Reserve to Hedges Road (southwest of Xenia)

Total Trail Miles (Certified): 49.5

Features: The trail meanders through rolling farm country, towering cliffs, and steep gorges. Forty seven miles of the trail is located in an old paved railroad bed. The trail follows the Little Miami River, a National and State Scenic River. Huge, towering sycamores, where great blue herons reside, border the edge of the river.

Partner Contact: Buckeye Trail Association, www.buckeyetrail.org

Local Information: Little Miami State Park & Caesar Creek State Park, 513-897-3055, www.dnr.state.oh.us/parks/parks/lilmiami.htm

Map Sources:
BTA, *Loveland Section & Caesar Creek Section**
NCTA, *Hutchins Guidebook - From Milford to Lake Loramie State Park (M304A)*

Segment 33: Little Miami Scenic Trail

Range: Hedges Road (southwest of Xenia) to I-70 (south of Springfield)

Total Trail Miles (Certified): 20.2

Features: The trail follows the Little Miami River, a state and national scenic river. This section is on a paved old Railroad bed.

Partner Contact: Buckeye Trail Association, www.buckeyetrail.org

Local Information: Greene County Parks and Recreation, 937-376-7440

Map Sources:
BTA, *Caesar Creek Section & Troy Section**
NCTA, *Hutchins Guidebook - From Milford to Lake Loramie State Park (M304A)*

Road Walk to Next Segment: 55 miles (not blazed)

Segment 34: Buckeye Trail

Range: Intersection of Statler and Troy Piqua Road (southeast of Piqua) to State
  Road 66 at Hardin Road
Total Trail Miles (Certified): 4.9
Road Walk to Next Segment: 0.5 miles (blazed)

Range: Hardin Road at Fence Row (N boundary of Johnston Farm) to Buckeye
  Trail at State Dam Road
Total Trail Miles (Not Certified): 1.5 miles
Road Walk to Next Segment: 2.0 miles (blazed)

Range: Fessler-Buxton Road (C-111) at Service Rd. (gated) to Towpath at Stan-
  gel Road (T-24)
Total Trail Miles (Not Certified): 2.2 miles
Road Walk to Next Segment: 5.8 miles (blazed)

Range: Pampel Road (C-128) at Miami Erie Towpath Trail to Miami Erie Towpath
  Trail at Stoker Road (T-120)
Total Trail Miles (Not Certified): 1.8 miles
Road Walk to Next Segment: 2.3 miles (blazed)

Range: Range Line Road (C-14) at Driveway on Towpath back to Range Line
  Road
Total Trail Miles (Not Certified): 0.2 miles
Road Walk to Next Segment: 0.1 miles (blazed)

Range: Range Line Road (C-14) at SR-47 and Towpath to Towpath at Loy Road
  (T-92)
Total Trail Miles (Not Certified): 2.7 miles
Road Walk to Next Segment: 2.5 miles (blazed)

Range: Schlater Road (C-102) at Residential Driveway on Towpath to SR-66 at
  SR-362 in Fort Loramie
Total Trail Miles (Not Certified): 1.1 miles
Road Walk to Next Segment: 2.0 miles (blazed)

Partner Contact: Buckeye Trail Association, www.buckeyetrail.org

Map Sources:
  BTA, *Troy Section & St. Marys Section**
  NCTA, *Hutchins Guidebook - From Milford to Lake Loramie State Park (M304A)*

Miami and Erie Canal Trail
Photo by Bill Menke

Segment 35: Miami and Erie Canal Trail

Range: State Road 362 in Lake Loramie State Park to Cleveland Street in Delphos

Total Trail Miles (Partially Certified): 36.9

Partner Contact: Buckeye Trail Association, www.buckeyetrail.org

Map Sources:
  BTA, *St. Marys Section* & *Delphos Section**
  NCTA, *Hutchins Guidebook - Following the Miami & Erie Canal from Lake Loramie State Park to Napoleon on the Buckeye Trail (M305A)*

Road Walk to Next Segment: 51.3 miles (blazed)

Segment 36: Independence Dam State Park

Range: State Park entrance at State Road 424 to new bridge over canal (1.4 miles east of Florida) *(Note: The trail is closed during eagle nesting season.)*

Total Trail Miles (Certified): 6.7

Features: The State Park is divided by the river on one side and the canal bed on the other side. It is mostly a wooded area with flat terrain and an abundance of woodland wildflowers. Eagles and turkeys as well as other types of songbirds can be seen.

Partner Contact: Buckeye Trail Association, www.buckeyetrail.org

Local Information: Independence Dam State Park
419-784-3263, www.dnr.state.oh.us/parks/parks/indpndam.htm

Map Sources:
BTA, *Defiance Section**
NCTA, *Hutchins Guidebook - Following the Miami & Erie Canal from Lake Loramie State Park to Napoleon on the Buckeye Trail (M305A)*

Road Walk to Next Segment: 17 miles (partially blazed)

Segment 37: Wabash Cannonball Trail

Range: State Highway 109 in Liberty Center to Berridge Road
Total Trail Miles (Partially Certified): 9.9
Road Walk to Next Segment: 5 miles (not blazed)

Range: Oak Openings Metropark to County Road 11
Total Trail Miles: 11.0
Road Walk to Next Segment: 3.5 miles (not blazed)

Range: Wauseon to Township Road 18
Total Trail Miles: 4.0
Road Walk to Next Segment: 7 miles (not blazed)

Range: State Highway 66 in Elmira to US Highway 20A
Total Trail Miles: 1.8

Features: This area of the trail is mainly farm land with a flatter terrain. A park is located at the eastern end of the trail. This land used to be part of black swamp where small sand islands developed. As a result, the woods are made up of trees and other associated plants that like moisture.

Partner Contact: Northwestern Ohio Rails to Trails Association (NORTA)
800-951-4788, http://home.tbbs.net/~norta/

Local Information: www.wabashcannonballtrail.org

Additional Information

* Regarding the maps from the Buckeye Trail Association (BTA), a complete set of section maps is available for $75.00 (a reduced price of $60.00 if you are a member of the Association.) For more information regarding maps or to purchase one or the entire set; visit www.buckeyetrail.org and go to the On Line store page and click on maps.

For more information regarding lodging, other types of accommodations, or other general tourism information about the state of Ohio call 1-800-BUCKEYE.

Since the North Country Trail weaves in and out of many of the State and National Forests; the features listed under one Segment do apply to all similarly titled Segments unless otherwise noted. For example all the Features listed under each segment of the Wayne National Forest apply to all Wayne National Forest segments.

Much of Ohio has the same variety of wildlife that can be seen primarily along forest waterway and would include, heron, loon, osprey, beaver and otter. In upland forests area, common mammals that could be seen include white-tailed deer, gray fox, woodchuck, opossum, and gray squirrel. Common birds such as turkey, ruffed grouse, pileated woodpecker and wood duck could be seen as well. This information was not listed under each segment but would apply to all.

Information regarding segments that share the trail with horseback riders: remember that if a horse is approaching you on the trail, you should stop hiking and stand on the uphill side of the trail and let the horse pass you. Individuals should speak so the horse knows you're a person, especially if you have a backpack. An example would be to just say hello or something.

Michigan

The trail enters Michigan and heads northwest passing through primarily agricultural lands as well as a variety of state and local recreation areas and uses local pathways. Continuing westward through Lowell and past the National Headquarters of the NCTA, the trail turns north and continues for 120 miles through the sandy-floored Manistee National Forest. Angling east through the Pere Marquette State Forest the trail joins the Shore-to-Shore Riding Hiking Trail. Turning north once again, the trail follows the western side of the peninsula passing through the scenic Jordan River Valley, state forest lands, and Wilderness State Park. The log stockades of Fort Michilimackinac stand guard at the tip of the Lower Peninsula as a living history

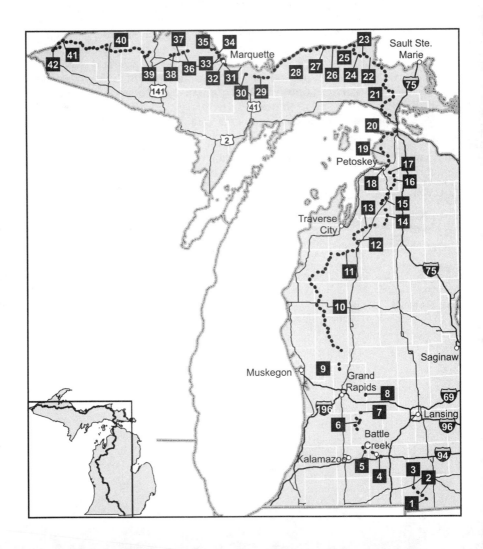

of French and British influence in the region. Use of a vehicle (a shuttle may be arranged) is necessary to cross the spectacular 5-mile long Mackinac Bridge except on Labor Day morning during the annual "Bridge Walk." Trail users will find a side trip to Mackinac Island enjoyable. At St. Ignace is the Father Marquette National Memorial. The trail then passes through the Hiawatha National Forest on its way to Tahquamenon Falls State Park, where the second largest waterfall east of the Mississippi River and many smaller falls await the hiker. Yet farther north the trail reaches Lake Superior just east of Muskallonge Lake State Park. The trail turns westward along Lake Superior to Pictured Rocks National Lakeshore. The 40-mile Lakeshore Trail along rock bluffs and sandy shores of Lake Superior provides outstanding vistas as well as primitive camping and hiking experiences (permit required for backcountry camping). Rock River Canyon Wilderness and Laughing Whitefish Falls provide outstanding scenery as the trail continues westward on more than 100 miles of off-road trail through the Ottawa National Forest and Porcupine Mountains Wilderness State Park. Rivers, waterfalls, forested hills and ridges characterize the trail. The trail leaves the state near Ironwood.

Segment 1: Lost Nation State Game Area

Range: Pittsford Road to Gilbert Road
Total Trail Miles: 3.2
Road Walk to Next Segment: 0.9 mile (not blazed)

Range: Reading Road to Tripp Road
Total Trail Miles: 1.2
Road Walk to Next Segment: 0.4 mile (not blazed)

Range: Tripp Road to Black Road
Total Trail Miles: 3.2
Road Walk to Next Segment: 2.1 miles (not blazed)

Local Volunteer Group: Baw Beese Chapter of NCTA
www.northcountrytrail.org/baw/index.htm/

Map Sources:
NCTA, *Johnson - Ohio State Line at Waldron to Augusta (M411A)*

Segment 2: Baw Beese Trail

Range: City of Hillsdale - Black Ridge Road (west of Osseo) to Bacon Street in Hillsdale

Total Trail Miles (Certified): 4.0

Features: The route goes through the grassy area to the south of the railroad grade. The railroad grade was once part of the Michigan Southern "Old Road", and was part of the first railroad connection between New York and Chicago.

Local Volunteer Group: Baw Beese Chapter of NCTA
www.northcountrytrail.org/baw/index.htm/

Local Information: Hillsdale County Chamber of Commerce
517-439-4341, www.hillsdalecountychamber.com/

Map Sources:
NCTA, *Johnson - Ohio State Line at Waldron to Augusta (M411A)*

Road Walk to Next Segment: 20 miles (not blazed)

Segment 3: State Highway 99 (M-99)Bikeway

Range: Carleton Road (northwest Hillsdale city limits) to Chicago Street (US 12) in Jonesville

Total Trail Miles (Certified): 5.0

Local Volunteer Group: Baw Beese Chapter of NCTA
www.northcountrytrail.org/baw/index.htm/

Map Sources:
NCTA, *Johnson - Ohio State Line at Waldron to Augusta (M411A)*

Road Walk to Next Segment: 40 miles (partially blazed)

Segment 4: Battle Creek and Surrounding Area

Range: Bridge Park (north of I-94 southeast of Battle Creek) to Kimball Pines (southeast of Battle Creek)
Total Trail Miles: 2.1
Road Walk to Next Segment: 1.0 mile (blazed)

Range: Ott Preserve (southeast of Battle Creek) to Jameson Street
Total Trail Miles: 1.2
Road Walk to Next Segment: 1.2 miles (blazed)

Range: Raymond Road to Armstrong Road
Total Trail Miles (Partially Certified): 9.9
Road Walk to Next Segment: 1 mile (not blazed)

Range: Fort Custer National Cemetery - Armstrong Road to Dickman Road
Total Trail Miles: 2.8
Road Walk to Next Segment: 0.3 mile (blazed)

Features: The trail winds through wooded areas, open fields, parks and even some commercial areas. There is an Underground Railroad monument along the Battle Creek Linear Park. Approximately 3.5 miles of this section pass through a remote portion of the 770 acre Fort Custer National Cemetery designated as such in 1943. This is a very pleasant hike through stands of red pine, old apple orchard, hardwoods and marsh areas.

Local Volunteer Group: Chief Noonday Chapter of NCTA
www.northcountrytrail.org/cnd/index.htm

Local Information: Battle Creek Area Chamber of Commerce
269-962-4076, www.battlecreek.org/chamber/index.html

Map Sources:
NCTA, *Johnson - Ohio State Line at Waldron to Augusta (M411A)*
NCTA, *Marshall to Bowne Township (MI-02)*
NCTA, *Battle Creek to Chief Noonday Road (T402)*

Augusta, Michigan
Photo by Tom Garnett

Segment 5: Augusta and North

Range: Kalamazoo River (east of Augusta) to State Highway 89 (including Kellogg Experimental Forest) *(Note: This segment crosses some private land.)*
Total Trail Miles (Certified): 4.0
Road Walk to Next Segment: 0.6 mile (blazed)

Range: State Highway 89 to 40th Street *(Note: This segment crosses some private land.)*
Total Trail Miles: 2.3
Road Walk to Next Segment: 0.1 mile (blazed)

Range: 40th Street to 39th Street
Total Trail Miles: 1.3
Road Walk to Next Segment: 15 miles (blazed)

Local Volunteer Group: Chief Noonday Chapter of NCTA
www.northcountrytrail.org/cnd/index.htm

Map Sources:
NCTA, *Johnson - Ohio State Line at Waldron to Augusta (M411A)*
NCTA, *Marshall to Bowne Township (MI-02)*
NCTA, *Battle Creek to Chief Noonday Road (T402)*

Segment 6: Barry State Game Area & Yankee Springs State Recreation Area

Range: Keller Road to McKibben Road *(Note: This segment crosses some private land.)*
Total Trail Miles: 0.8
Road Walk to Next Segment: 0.5 mile (blazed)

Range: Mullen Road to Bowens Mill Road
Total Trail Miles (Partially Certified): 12.3
Road Walk to Next Segment: 0.5 mile (not blazed)

Range: Bowens Mill Road to Peets Road
Total Trail Miles (Certified): 0.7
Road Walk to Next Segment: 0.4 mile (not blazed)

Range: Peets Road to Peets Road
Total Trail Miles (Certified): 0.6
Road Walk to Next Segment: 2.0 miles (blazed)

Features: Yankee Springs Recreation Area was once the hunting grounds of the Algonquin Indians and the famous Chieftain, Chief Noonday. Within the park's 5,000 acres, some of the terrain is rugged. There are bogs and marshes, and streams, as well as nine lakes. Forests are composed of over seventy species of native trees.

Local Volunteer Group: Chief Noonday Chapter of NCTA
www.northcountrytrail.org/cnd/index.htm

Local Information: Barry State Game Area, 269-795-3280

Yankee Springs State Recreation Area, 269-795-9081,
www.michigandnr.com/parksandtrails/parksandtrailsinfo.asp?id=511

Map Sources:
NCTA, *Johnson - Augusta to Rogue River State Game Area (M412A)*
NCTA, *Marshall to Bowne Township (MI-02)*
NCTA, *Battle Creek to Chief Noonday Road (T402)*

Segment 7: Paul Henry Trail

Range: Cann Road (south of Irving) to Main Street (Middleville)

Total Trail Miles: 3.7

Local Volunteer Group: Chief Noonday Chapter of NCTA
www.northcountrytrail.org/cnd/index.htm

Map Sources:
NCTA, *Johnson - Augusta to Rogue River State Game Area (M412A)*
NCTA, *Marshall to Bowne Township (MI-02)*

Road Walk to Next Segment: 21 miles (blazed)

Segment 8: Lowell,
Lowell State Game Area & Fallasburg Park

Range: Grand River Drive to Montcalm Avenue
Total Trail Miles (Certified): 5.8
Road Walk to Next Segment: 0.9 miles (not blazed)

Range: Covered Bridge Road to McPherson Street (Fallasburg Park)
Total Trail Miles (Certified): 0.8
Road Walk to Next Segment: 35 miles (not blazed)

Features: This area has a variety of landscapes from sand dunes with leftover glacial rocks to a tall red pine forest to a scrubby jack pine grove to different hardwood forests.

Local Volunteer Group: Western Michigan Chapter of NCTA
www.northcountrytrail.org/wmi/index.htm

Local Information: DNR Wildlife Field Office (Lowell State Game Area)
616-794-2658, www.michigan.gov/dnr/

Lowell Chamber of Commerce
616-897-9161, www.lowellchamber.org

Map Sources:
NCTA, *Johnson - Augusta to Rogue River State Game Area (M412A)*
NCTA, *Bowne Township to M-37 (MI-03)*

Lowell, Michigan
Photo by Aaron Phipps

Segment 9: Rogue River State Game Area

Range: 17 Mile Road (State Hwy 57) to Solon Road *(Note: This segment crosses some private land.)*
Total Trail Miles (Certified): 0.8
Road Walk to Next Segment: 1.0 miles (not blazed)

Range: Division Avenue to pipeline *(Note: This segment crosses some private land.)*
Total Trail Miles (Certified): 0.5
Road Walk to Next Segment: 0.8 mile (not blazed)

Range: Two-track off the west side of Red Pine Drive to 18 Mile Road
Total Trail Miles (Certified): 0.5
Road Walk to Next Segment: 0.5 mile (blazed)

Range: Red Pine Drive to 22 Mile Road *(Note: This segment crosses some private land.)*
Total Trail Miles (Certified): 5.6
Road Walk to Next Segment: 14 miles (not blazed)

Local Volunteer Group: Western Michigan Chapter of NCTA
www.northcountrytrail.org/wmi/index.htm

Local Information: Rogue River State Game Area
(616) 788-5055, www.michigan.gov/dnr/

Map Sources:
NCTA, *Johnson - Augusta to Rogue River State Game Area (M412A)*
NCTA, *Bowne Township to M-37 (MI-03)*

Segment 10: Manistee National Forest

Range: Croton Dam to 56th Street
Total Trail Miles (Certified): 2.0
Road Walk to Next Segment: 0.1 mile (not blazed)

Range: 56th Street to woods road in the southwest corner of Section 1 (T12N, R12W)
Total Trail Miles (Certified): 0.3
Road Walk to Next Segment: 0.4 mile (blazed)

Range: Woods road in the southwest corner of Section 1 (T12N, R12W) to Spruce Avenue
Total Trail Miles (Certified): 3.4
Road Walk to Next Segment: 1.9 miles (blazed)

Range: 40th Street in Newaygo County to Centerline Road
Total Trail Miles (Certified): 8.4
Road Walk to Next Segment: 0.7 mile (blazed)

Range: Echo Drive to 40th Street in Lake County
Total Trail Miles (Certified): 46.4
Road Walk to Next Segment: 0.5 mile (not blazed)

Range: 40th Street in Lake County to 5 Mile Road (north of Sauble)
Total Trail Miles (Certified): 17.9
Road Walk to Next Segment: 2.3 miles (not blazed)

Range: 5 Mile Road (north of Sauble) to Riverside Drive (south of Little Manistee River)
Total Trail Miles (Certified): 11.9
Road Walk to Next Segment: 0.9 mile (not blazed)

Range: Udell Hills Road to Huff Road (just north of State Hwy 55)
Total Trail Miles (Partially Certified): 7.2
Road Walk to Next Segment: 3.0 miles (blazed)

Range: Chicago Avenue to No.16 Road (west of Mesick), also includes nearly 1 mile in Pere Marquette State Forest
Total Trail Miles (Certified): 24.7
Road Walk to Next Segment: 1.7 miles (not blazed)

Features: A hiker can see it all in the National Forest from the most challenging to the easiest hike. Areas can be open woodlands and forests while others areas are flat, while still others have rolling hills. Highlights are the several beautiful rivers and streams.

Local Volunteer Groups: Western Michigan Chapter of NCTA
www.northcountrytrail.org/wmi/index.htm

Spirit of the Woods Chapter of NCTA
www.northcountrytrail.org/spw/index.htm

Grand Traverse Hiking Club Chapter of NCTA
www.northcountrytrail.org/gtr/index.htm

Local Information: Huron-Manistee National Forest (Baldwin Ranger District)
231-745-4631, www.fs.fed.us/r9/hmnf

Manistee National Forest (Manistee Ranger District)
231-723-2211, www.fs.fed.us/r9/hmnf

Map Sources:
NCTA, *Bowne Township to M-37 (MI-03)*
NCTA, *Freesoil Trailhead to Cedar Creek Road (MI-05)*
NCTA, *Huron-Manistee National Forest South Segment (T403)*
NCTA, *Huron-Manistee National Forest North Segment (T401)*
NCTA, *Johnson - Rogue River State Game Area to M-115 West of Mesick (M413A)*
NCTA, *Hutchins Guidebook - NCT in Lower Michigan (M401)*

Manistee National Forest
Photo by Eric Doyle

Segment 11: Pere Marquette State Forest

Range: West No.14 Road (west of Mesick) to No.8 Road
Total Trail Miles (Partially Certified): 3.6
Road Walk to Next Segment: 5.5 miles (not blazed)

Range: Road just west of Wheeler Creek to road in southeast corner of Section 19 (just east of Wheeler Creek)
Total Trail Miles (Certified): 0.6
Road Walk to Next Segment: 0.8 mile (blazed)

Range: Road near SW corner of Section 20 (east of Wheeler Creek) to No.29 ½ Road (south of Baxter)
Total Trail Miles (Partially Certified): 10.8
Road Walk to Next Segment: 2.6 miles (not blazed)

Range: Dell Road (northeast of Baxter) to Hellister Road (east of Walton)
Total Trail Miles (Partially Certified): 12.7
Road Walk to Next Segment: 1.7 miles (not blazed)

Features: There are an abundance of rivers and streams with the terrain level to rolling. The vegetation is varied but the forests are composed of pines and hardwoods. Hawks and bald eagle can be seen along with, bear, deer, raccoon and squirrel. Various song and game birds are also visible.

Local Volunteer Group: Grand Traverse Hiking Club Chapter of NCTA
www.northcountrytrail.org/gtr/index.htm

Local Information: Pere Marquette State Forest, MI DNR (Cadillac)
231-775-9727, www.michigan.gov/dnr/

Map Sources:
NCTA, *Freesoil Trailhead to Cedar Creek Road (MI-05)*
NCTA, *Johnson - M-115 West of Mesick to M-32 West of US 131 (M414A)*
NCTA, *Hutchins Guidebook - NCT in Lower Michigan (M401)*

Segment 12: Southern Spur of Shore-To-Shore Trail

Range: Revord Road and US Hwy 131 (north of Walton) to Sheck's Place State Forest Campground (in and out of Pere Marquette State Forest)

Total Trail Miles (Partially Certified): 10.7

Features: There are an abundance of rivers and streams with the terrain level to rolling. The vegetation is varied but the forests are composed of pines and hardwoods. Wildlife can be seen. Various birds are also visible.

Local Volunteer Group: Grand Traverse Hiking Club Chapter of NCTA www.northcountrytrail.org/gtr/index.htm

Local Information: Pere Marquette State Forest, MI DNR (Cadillac) 231-775-9727, www.michigan.gov/dnr/

Michigan Trail Riders Association (Horses), 517-851-7554, www.mtra.org

Map Sources:
NCTA, *Freesoil Trailhead to Cedar Creek Road (MI-05)*
NCTA, *Cedar Creek Road to Charlevoix County (MI-06)*
NCTA, *Johnson - M-115 West of Mesick to M-32 West of US 131 (M414A)*
NCTA, *Hutchins Guidebook - NCT in Lower Michigan (M401)*

Segment 13: Shore-To-Shore Trail – Pere Marquette State Forest

Range: Sheck's Place State Forest Campground (Pere Marquette State Forest) to Aller Road (northeast of Kalkaska)

Total Trail Miles (Certified): 23.4

Features: There are an abundance of rivers and streams with the terrain level to rolling. The vegetation is varied but the forests are composed of pines and hardwoods. Wildlife can be seen. Various birds are also visible.

Local Volunteer Group: Grand Traverse Hiking Club Chapter of NCTA www.northcountrytrail.org/gtr/index.htm

Local Information: Pere Marquette State Forest, Michigan DNR (Cadillac) 231-775-9727, www.michigan.gov/dnr/

Michigan Trail Riders Association (Horses) 517-851-7554, www.mtra.org

Map Sources:
NCTA, *Cedar Creek Road to Charlevoix County (MI-06)*
NCTA, *Johnson - M-115 West of Mesick to M-32 West of US 131 (M414A)*
NCTA, *Hutchins Guidebook - NCT in Lower Michigan (M401)*

Road Walk to Next Segment: 7.5 miles (not blazed)

Segment 14: Pere Marquette & Mackinaw State Forests

Range: Manistee Lake Road (east of Darragh) to the two-track north of Sand Lake (east of Mancelona)
Total Trail Miles (Partially Certified): 10.1
Road Walk to Next Segment: 1.5 miles (blazed)

Range: Mancelona Road (east of Mancelona) to Doerr Road (south of Alba)
Total Trail Miles (Certified): 5.5
Road Walk to Next Segment: 4.0 miles (blazed)

Features: Northern hardwood forests, lowland conifer swamps, small game, deer, bear habitat, coyote, birds, orchids.

Local Volunteer Group: Tittabawassee Chapter of NCTA
www.northcountrytrail.org/tbw/index.htm

Local Information: Pere Marquette State Forest, Michigan DNR (Cadillac) 231-775-9727, www.michigan.gov/dnr/

Mackinaw State Forest, Michigan DNR (Gaylord) 989-732-3541, www.michigan.gov/dnr/

Map Sources:
NCTA, *Cedar Creek Road to Charlevoix County (MI-06)*
NCTA, *Johnson - M-115 West of Mesick to M-32 West of US 131 (M414A)*
NCTA, *Hutchins Guidebook - NCT in Lower Michigan (M401)*

Segment 15: Jordan River Valley Pathway, Warner Creek Pathway & Mackinaw State Forest

Range: Harvey Road (northeast of Alba) to State Highway 32 (west of Elmira)

Total Trail Miles (Certified): 12.3

Features: The Jordan River Pathway, a state recreation trail

Local Volunteer Group: Tittabawassee Chapter of NCTA
www.northcountrytrail.org/tbw/index.htm

Local Information: Mackinaw State Forest, Michigan DNR (Gaylord) 989-732-3541, www.michigan.gov/dnr/

Map Sources:
NCTA, *Cedar Creek Road to Charlevoix County (MI-06)*
NCTA, *Johnson - M-115 West of Mesick to M-32 West of US 131 (M414A)*
NCTA, *Hutchins Guidebook - NCT in Lower Michigan (M401)*

Road Walk to Next Segment: 0.4 miles (blazed)

Segment 16: Mackinaw State Forest

Range: Two-track road in southwest corner of Section 9 north of State Hwy 32 (west of Elmira) to two-track in southwest corner of Section 9 north of State Hwy 32 (northwest of Elmira)
Total Trail Miles (Certified): 0.4
Road Walk to Next Segment: 1.4 miles (blazed)

Range: Two-track on section line between Sections 10 and 11 (northwest of Elmira) to Dobleski Road (northwest of Elmira)
Total Trail Miles (Partially Certified): 0.8
Road Walk to Next Segment: 2.4 miles (blazed)

Range: Giem Road (between Elmira and Boyne Falls) to Licks Creek (east of Boyne Falls)
Total Trail Miles: 2.9
Road Walk to Next Segment: 5.1 miles (blazed)

Range: Slashing Road north of Thumb Lake Road (County Road 48) to Harmon Road (northwest of Springvale)
Total Trail Miles (Partially Certified): 11.0
Road Walk to Next Segment: 1.2 miles (blazed)

Features: Northern hardwood forests, lowland conifer swamps, with a few unusual orchids. There are small game animals, deer, coyote, and various kinds of birds.

Local Volunteer Group: Tittabawassee Chapter of NCTA
www.northcountrytrail.org/tbw/index.htm

Local Information: Mackinaw State Forest, Michigan DNR (Gaylord)
989-732-3541, www.michigan.gov/dnr/

Map Sources:
NCTA, *Cedar Creek Road to Charlevoix County (MI-06)*
NCTA, *Charlevoix County to Mackinac Bridge (MI-07)*
NCTA, *Johnson - M-32 West of of US 131 to Mackinaw City (M415A)*
NCTA, *Hutchins Guidebook - NCT in Lower Michigan (M401)*

Segment 17: Mackinaw State Forest – Petoskey Area

Range: Taylor Road (southeast of Petosky) to Krause Road (southeast of Petoskey)
Total Trail Miles (Partially Certified): 4.1
Road Walk to Next Segment: 0.5 mile (blazed)

Range: Krause Road to Brubaker Road (southeast of Petoskey)
Total Trail Miles (Certified): 0.6
Road Walk to Next Segment: 3.1 miles (blazed)

Features: Northern hardwood forests, lowland conifer swamps, with a few unusual orchids. There are small game animals, deer, coyote, and various kinds of birds.

Local Volunteer Group: Tittabawassee Chapter of NCTA
www.northcountrytrail.org/tbw/index.htm

Local Information: Mackinaw State Forest, Michigan DNR (Gaylord)
989-732-3541, www.michigan.gov/dnr/

Map Sources:
NCTA, *Charlevoix County to Mackinac Bridge (MI-07)*
NCTA, *Johnson - M-32 West of of US 131 to Mackinaw City (M415A)*
NCTA, *Hutchins Guidebook - NCT in Lower Michigan (M401)*

Segment 18: Petoskey Area

Range: McDougal Road (southeast of Petoskey) to Howard Street (includes North Central Michigan College)
Total Trail Miles (Certified): 1.7
Road Walk to Next Segment: 0.7 miles (blazed)

Range: Sheridan Road (Petoskey) to North Conway Road (north of Conway)
Total Trail Miles (Partially Certified): 7.1
Road Walk to Next Segment: 2.0 miles (blazed)

Local Volunteer Group: Tittabawassee Chapter of NCTA
www.northcountrytrail.org/tbw/index.htm

Local Information: North Central Michigan College
888-298-6605, www.ncmc.cc.mi.us/

Map Sources:
NCTA, *Charlevoix County to Mackinac Bridge (MI-07)*
NCTA, *Johnson - M-32 West of of US 131 to Mackinaw City (M415A)*
NCTA, *Hutchins Guidebook - NCT in Lower Michigan (M401)*

Segment 19: Mackinaw State Forest

Range: Kipp Road (west of North Conway Road) to Stutzmanville Road (east of Pleasant View)
Total Trail Miles: 4.7
Road Walk to Next Segment: 2.0 mile (blazed)

Range: Stutzmanville Road (west of Pleasant View Road) to Van Road
Total Trail Miles: 7.4
Road Walk to Next Segment: 6.0 mile (blazed)

Range: Levering Road (west of Pleasant View Road) to Wilderness State Park (just south of Sturgeon Bay Trail)
Total Trail Miles: 4.5

Features: Northern hardwood forests, lowland conifer swamps, with a few unusual orchids. There are small game animals, deer, coyote, and various kinds of birds. In addition, Wycamp Lake, sand dunes and a sandy pine forest are located in the forest.

Local Volunteer Group: Habor Springs Chapter of NCTA
www.northcountrytrail.org/hrb/index.htm

Local Information: Mackinaw State Forest, Michigan DNR (Gaylord)
989-732-3541, www.michigan.gov/dnr/

Map Sources:
NCTA, *Charlevoix County to Mackinac Bridge (MI-07)*
NCTA, *Johnson - M-32 West of of US 131 to Mackinaw City (M415A)*
NCTA, *Hutchins Guidebook - NCT in Lower Michigan (M401)*

Hiawatha National Forest
Photo by Roger Morrison

Segment 20: Wilderness State Park – Mackinaw State Forest

Range: South Park boundary (just south of Sturgeon Bay Trail) to French Farm Lake Road (southwest of Mackinaw City)

Total Trail Miles (Certified): 18.5

Features: Rare and endangered wildflowers such as the calypso orchid. Miles of shoreline and some excellent fishing spots for small mouth bass. The area is more flat than hilly but has plenty of natural beauty. Some examples of wildlife would be bobcat, coyote, fox, and birds such as eagles.

Local Volunteer Group: Habor Springs Chapter of NCTA
www.northcountrytrail.org/hrb/index.htm

Local Information: Wilderness State Park, 231-436-5381
www.michigandnr.com/parksandtrails/parksandtrailsinfo.asp?id=509

Mackinaw State Forest, Michigan DNR (Gaylord)
989-732-3541, www.michigan.gov/dnr/

Map Sources:
NCTA, *Charlevoix County to Mackinac Bridge (MI-07)*
NCTA, *Johnson - M-32 West of of US 131 to Mackinaw City (M415A)*
NCTA, *Hutchins Guidebook - NCT in Lower Michigan (M401)*

Road Walk to Next Segment: 15 miles (not blazed)

Segment 21: Hiawatha National Forest - East Unit

Range: Forest Road 3104 (northwest of St. Ignace) to north Forest Boundary (southeast of State Hwy 123)

Total Trail Miles (Certified): 77.4

Features: Mainly rolling country, with forests of northern hardwoods, pine, spruce, and fir. Numerous lakes, streams, and wetlands are to be found, and the trail passes several campgrounds. For several miles it follows the Lake Superior shoreline, with wide, sandy beaches.

Local Volunteer Group: Hiawatha Shore-to-Shore Chapter of NCTA
www.northcountrytrail.org/hss/index.htm

Local Information: Hiawatha National Forest
906-643-7900 (St. Ignace Ranger Station)
906-635-5311 (Sault Ste Marie Ranger Station)
www.fs.fed.us/r9/forests/hiawatha/

Map Sources:
NCTA, *Johnson - St. Ignace to Marquette (M416A)*
NCTA, *Hutchins Guidebook - NCT in Upper Michigan (M402)*

Road Walk to Next Segment: 10 miles (partially blazed)

Segment 22: Tahquamenon Falls State Park

Range: State Hwy 123 to West Park boundary (in Section 2 northwest of the Upper Falls)

Total Trail Miles: 15.4

Features: Tahquamenon Falls State Park encompasses close to 40,000 acres stretching over 13 miles. Most of this is undeveloped woodland without roads, buildings or power lines. The centerpiece of the park, and the very reason for its existence, is the Tahquamenon River, with its waterfalls.

Local Volunteer Group: Hiawatha Shore-to-Shore Chapter of NCTA www.northcountrytrail.org/hss/index.htm

Local Information: Tahquamenon Falls State Park, 906-492-3415 www.michigandnr.com/parksandtrails/parksandtrailsinfo.asp?id=428

Map Sources:
NCTA, *Curley Lewis Road to Grand Marais (MI-09)*
NCTA, *Johnson - St. Ignace to Marquette (M416A)*
NCTA, *Hutchins Guidebook - NCT in Upper Michigan (M402)*

Segment 23: Lake Superior State Forest

Range: Tahquamenon Falls/Lake Superior State Forest boundary (in Section 2 northwest of the Upper Falls) to Tahquamenon Falls/Lake Superior State Forest boundary(line between sections 4 and 33)

Total Trail Miles (Certified): 3.0

Features: Mostly gently rolling country, with forests of northern hardwoods, pine, spruce, and fir. Numerous lakes, streams, and wetlands.

Local Volunteer Group: Hiawatha Shore-to-Shore Chapter of NCTA www.northcountrytrail.org/hss/index.htm

Local Information: Lake Superior State Forest, Michigan DNR (Marquette) 906-228-6561, www.michigan.gov/dnr/

Map Sources:
NCTA, *Curley Lewis Road to Grand Marais (MI-09)*
NCTA, *Johnson - St. Ignace to Marquette (M416A)*

Segment 24: Tahquamenon Falls State Park

Range: Tahquamenon Falls/Lake Superior State Forest boundary (line between Section 4 and 33) to two-track road east of County Road 500(southeast of the Little Two Hearted River) *(Note: This segment crosses some private land.)*

Total Trail Miles (Partially Certified): 1.6

Local Volunteer Group: Hiawatha Shore-to-Shore Chapter of NCTA
www.northcountrytrail.org/hss/index.htm

Local Information: Tahquamenon Falls State Park, 906-492-3415
www.michigandnr.com/parksandtrails/parksandtrailsinfo.asp?id=428

Map Sources:
NCTA, *Curley Lewis Road to Grand Marais (MI-09)*
NCTA, *Johnson - St. Ignace to Marquette (M416A)*

Road Walk to Next Segment: 1.0 mile (blazed)

Segment 25: Lake Superior State Forest

Range: Two-track west of County Road 500 (just north of the Little Two Hearted River) to two-track in Section 6 (south of Dry Lakes) *(Note: This segment crosses some private land.)*
Total Trail Miles (Certified): 6.8
Road Walk to Next Segment: 0.4 mile (blazed)

Range: Two-track road east of Dry Lakes in Section 6 to two-track road north of Dry Lakes in Section 6
Total Trail Miles (Certified): 0.3
Road Walk to Next Segment: 0.2 mile (blazed)

Range: Two-track north of Dry Lakes in Section 6 to County Road 412 near the mouth of the Little Two Hearted River
Total Trail Miles (Partially Certified): 3.6
Road Walk to Next Segment: 0.2 mile (blazed)

Range: County Road 412 near the mouth of the Little Two Hearted River to two-track in the northwest corner of Section 1 (northeast of the Reed and Green Bridge Campground)
Total Trail Miles (Certified): 8.1
Road Walk to Next Segment: 0.2 mile (blazed)

Range: Two-track in the northwest corner of Section 1 (northeast of the Reed and Green Bridge Campground) to Coast Guard Road
Total Trail Miles (Certified): 0.5
Road Walk to Next Segment: 1.6 miles (blazed)

Range: Two track between Sections 2 & 3 (northwest of the Reed and Green Bridge Campground) to Coast Guard Road
Total Trail Miles (Certified): 1.4
Road Walk to Next Segment: 0.5 mile (blazed)

Range: Two-track in Section 4 (north of Coast Guard Road) to two-track be-
tween Sections 3 & 4 (north of Coast Guard Road)
Total Trail Miles (Certified): 0.8
Road Walk to Next Segment: 0.6 mile (blazed)

Range: Coast Guard Road (Section 5) to Coast Guard Road (between sections
5 & 6)
Total Trail Miles (Certified): 1.0
Road Walk to Next Segment: 0.2 mile (blazed)

Range: Coast Guard Road to H-37 in Deer Park
Total Trail Miles (Certified): 1.1
Road Walk to Next Segment: 0.3 mile (blazed)

Features: The terrain throughout this area is mixed, but mostly made up of mature forests, sand dunes and blueberries. The trail follows the Lake Superior
shoreline.

Local Volunteer Group: Hiawatha Shore-to-Shore Chapter of NCTA
www.northcountrytrail.org/hss/index.htm

Grand Marias Chapter of NCTA
www.northcountrytrail.org/gmc/index.htm

Local Information: Lake Superior State Forest, Michigan DNR (Marquette)
906-228-6561, www.michigan.gov/dnr/

Map Sources:
NCTA, *Curley Lewis Road to Grand Marais (MI-09)*
NCTA, *Johnson - St. Ignace to Marquette (M416A)*

Segment 26: Muskallonge Lake State Park

Range: H-37 to H-58 at west park boundary

Total Trail Miles (Certified): 1.5

Features: The 217-acre park is situated between the shores of Lake Superior
and Muskallonge Lake and the area is well known for its forests, lakes, and
streams.

Local Volunteer Group: Grand Marias Chapter of NCTA
www.northcountrytrail.org/gmc/index.htm

Local Information: Muskallonge Lake State Park, 906-658-3338
www.michigandnr.com/parksandtrails/parksandtrailsinfo.asp?id=424

Map Sources:
NCTA, *Curley Lewis Road to Grand Marais (MI-09)*
NCTA, *Johnson - St. Ignace to Marquette (M416A)*

Road Walk to Next Segment: 0.3 mile (blazed)

Segment 27: Lake Superior State Forest

Range: H-58 at west side of Muskellonge Lake SP to two-track in northwest corner of Section 3 (north of Mud Lake)
Total Trail Miles (Certified): 1.3
Road Walk to Next Segment: 0.5 mile (blazed)

Range: Two-track in northeast corner of section 4 (northwest of Mud Lake) to two-track in southwest corner of Section 3 (north of Dead Sucker River)
Total Trail Miles (Certified): 6.9
Road Walk to Next Segment: 0.1 mile (blazed)

Range: Two-track in southwest corner of Section 3 (north of Dead Sucker River) to two-track in east half of Section 35 (north of the Sucker River)
Total Trail Miles (Certified): 6.6
Road Walk to Next Segment: 0.3 mile (blazed)

Range: Two-track in east half of Section 35 (north of the Sucker River) to dirt road south of H-58 in Section 9
Total Trail Miles (Certified): 4.5
Road Walk to Next Segment: 0.3 mile (blazed)

Range: Two-track between Sections 4 and 9 (east of Grand Marais) to H-58 east of Grand Marais (in Section 4)
Total Trail Miles (Certified): 0.3
Road Walk to Next Segment: 3.0 miles (blazed)

Features: This area features mature forest, sand dunes and lots of blueberries as well. The trail takes advantage of older sand dunes that support pine trees, so the footing is firm and views are lovely. There are several easy access points from the trail down to the beach. The terrain varies from hilly to rolling and takes advantage of the vast sand dunes that mark the south shore of Lake Superior.

Local Volunteer Group: Grand Marias Chapter of NCTA
www.northcountrytrail.org/gmc/index.htm

Local Information: Lake Superior State Forest, Michigan DNR (Marquette)
906-228-6561, www.michigan.gov/dnr/

Map Sources:
NCTA, *Curley Lewis Road to Grand Marais (MI-09)*
NCTA, *Johnson - St. Ignace to Marquette (M416A)*

Segment 28: Pictured Rocks National Lakeshore

Range: Brazel Street in Grand Marais (west of Woodland Park) to Munising Falls Visitors Center (also includes 0.3 miles just east of Pictured Rocks)

Total Trail Miles (Partially Certified): 44.6

Features: 73,000+ acre park includes multicolored sandstone cliffs, intriguing rock formations, beaches, sand dunes, waterfalls and inland lakes. Falcons often fly above cliffs and the views are dramatic. Attractions include a lighthouse and former Coast Guard life-saving stations along with old farmsteads and former logging trails.

Local Volunteer Group: Grand Marias Chapter of NCTA
www.northcountrytrail.org/gmc/index.htm

Local Information: Pictured Rocks National Lakeshore & Hiawatha National Forest
906-387-3700 (Pictured Rocks Visitor Center)
906 387-2512 (Hiawatha National Forest), www.fs.fed.us/r9/forests/hiawatha/

Map Sources:
NCTA, *Grand Marais to Au Train Lake (MI-10)*
NCTA, *Johnson - St. Ignace to Marquette (M416A)*
NCTA, *Hutchins Guidebook - NCT in Upper Michigan (M402)*

Road Walk to Next Segment: 5.0 miles (blazed)

Segment 29: Hiawatha National Forest - West Unit

Range: M-94 in Section 16 (south of Munising) to County Road H-01 (east edge of Rock River Canyon Wilderness)

Total Trail Miles (Certified): 16.1

Features: Stands of hardwoods and pines with varied terrain. There are many lakes and rivers. Many different kinds of birds as well as black bear and wolves make their home in the National Forest.

Local Volunteer Group: Grand Marias Chapter of NCTA
www.northcountrytrail.org/gmc/index.htm

Local Information: Pictured Rocks National Lakeshore & Hiawatha National Forest
906-387-3700 (Pictured Rocks Visitor Center)
906 387-2512 (Hiawatha National Forest), www.fs.fed.us/r9/forests/hiawatha/

Map Sources:
NCTA, *Grand Marais to Au Train Lake (MI-10)*
NCTA, *Au Train Lake to Little Garlic Falls (MI-11)*
NCTA, *Johnson - St. Ignace to Marquette (M416A)*
NCTA, *Hutchins Guidebook - NCT in Upper Michigan (M402)*

Road Walk to Next Segment: 6.0 miles (not blazed)

Pictured Rocks National Lakeshore
Photo by Neil Rinne

Segment 30: Laughing Whitefish Falls State Scenic Site & Surrounding Area

Range: West boundary of Rock River Canyon Wilderness to Rumley Road
Total Trail Miles: 3.1
Road Walk to Next Segment: 0.9 mile (blazed)

Range: Rumley Road to Sigan Road *(Note: This segment crosses some private land.)*
Total Trail Miles: 5.6
Road Walk to Next Segment: 1.5 miles (blazed)

Range: Sigan Road to Escanaba River State Forest (near center of Section 30 northwest of Howe Lake)
Total Trail Miles: 0.2

Features: Passes through the northern portion of Laughing Whitefish Falls State Scenic Site. A spur trail of approximately two miles can be taken to Laughing Whitefish Falls.

Local Volunteer Group: North Country Trail Hikers Chapter of NCTA
www.northcountrytrail.org/nct/index.htm

Local Information: Laughing Whitefish Falls State Scenic Site
www.michigandnr.com/parksandtrails/parksandtrailsinfo.asp?id=422

Map Sources:
NCTA, *Au Train Lake to Little Garlic Falls (MI-11)*
NCTA, *Johnson - St. Ignace to Marquette (M416A)*

Segment 31: Escanaba River State Forest

Range: Near center of Section 30 (northwest of Howe Lake) to Sand River Road
Total Trail Miles (Certified): 2.6
Road Walk to Next Segment: 0.7 mile (not blazed)

Range: Sand River Road to near old Soo Line Railroad (west of Sand Lake in Section 12)
Total Trail Miles (Certified): 0.8
Road Walk to Next Segment: 12.5 miles (not blazed)

Features: Rolling hardwood hills east of Sand River Road, with pine-covered sand plains to the west.

Local Volunteer Group: North Country Trail Hikers Chapter of NCTA www.northcountrytrail.org/nct/index.htm

Local Information: Escanaba River State Forest, Michigan DNR (Marquette) 906-228-6561, www.michigan.gov/dnr/

Map Sources: NCTA, *Au Train Lake to Little Garlic Falls (MI-11)*

Segment 32: Marquette Bike Path

Range: Southeast City Limit near lakeshore (between Sections 36 and 1) to Road just north of the Carp River
Total Trail Miles (Certified): 1.3
Road Walk to Next Segment: 1.9 miles (blazed)

Range: South boundary of Mattson Park to Hawley Street extension of bike path
Total Trail Miles (Certified): 3.1
Road Walk to Next Segment: 0.2 miles (blazed)

Features: Mostly sidewalk along the scenic Lake Superior shoreline. There is convenient access to downtown businesses.

Local Volunteer Group: North Country Trail Hikers Chapter of NCTA www.northcountrytrail.org/nct/index.htm

Local Information: Marquette Country Convention & Visitors Bureau 800-544-4321 or 906-228-7749, www.marquettecountry.org/

Marquette Chamber of Commerce, www.marquette.org/

Map Sources:
NCTA, *Au Train Lake to Little Garlic Falls (MI-11)*
NCTA, *Johnson - St. Ignace to Marquette (M416A)*
NCTA, *Johnson - Marquette to Ironwood (M417A)*

Segment 33: Marquette to
Little Presque Isle State Recreation Area

Range: Hawley Street extension of bike path to Forestville Road
Total Trail Miles: 4.0
Road Walk to Next Segment: 0.8 mile (not blazed)

Range: Forestville Road to powerline road
Total Trail Miles: 0.2
Road Walk to Next Segment: 0.2 mile (blazed)

Range: Powerline Road to Little Presque Isle State Recreation Area
Total Trail Miles: 1.3

Local Volunteer Group: North Country Trail Hikers Chapter of NCTA
www.northcountrytrail.org/nct/index.htm

Map Sources: NCTA, *Au Train Lake to Little Garlic Falls (MI-11)*

Segment 34: Little Presque Isle State Recreation Area

Range: Little Presque Isle boundary in the southeast corner of Section 30 to Little Presque Isle boundary between Sections 13 and 14 (northwest of Marquette)

Total Trail Miles (Partially Certified): 7.1

Features: This area is often called the crown jewel of Lake Superior. This segment rambles through this stunningly beautiful area renowned for its vast sand beaches, rugged shoreline cliffs, heavily timbered forests and unmatched views. The State Recreation Area is 3,000 acres and boasts numerous cold water trout streams, and side trails to high overlooks. Deer and songbirds abound.

Local Volunteer Group: North Country Trail Hikers Chapter of NTCA
www.northcountrytrail.org/nct/index.htm

Local Information: Escanaba River State Forest, Michigan DNR (Marquette)
906-228-6561, www.michigan.gov/dnr/

Map Sources:
NCTA, *Au Train Lake to Little Garlic Falls (MI-11)*
NCTA, *Johnson - Marquette to Ironwood (M417A)*

Road Walk to Next Segment: 3.6 miles (not blazed)

Segment 35: Escanaba River State Forest – Little Garlic River

Range: County Road 550 to Woods Road just west of Little Garlic Falls

Total Trail Miles: 3.7

Features: This trail segment runs through mixed forest following the Little Garlic River. The western section ends at a beautiful waterfall.

Local Volunteer Group: North Country Trail Hikers Chapter of NTCA www.northcountrytrail.org/nct/index.htm

Local Information: Escanaba River State Forest, Michigan DNR (Marquette) 906-228-6561, www.michigan.gov/dnr/

Map Sources:
NCTA, *Au Train Lake to Little Garlic Falls (MI-11)*
NCTA, *Johnson - Marquette to Ironwood (M417A)*
NCTA, *Hutchins Guidebook - NCT in Upper Michigan (M402)*

Road Walk to Next Segment: 50 miles (not blazed)

Little Garlic River
Photo by Neil Rinne

Segment 36: Ottawa National Forest – McCormick Wilderness/McCormick Tract

Range: East boundary of McCormick Wilderness (southeast of Lake Raymond) to southwest boundary of McCormick Tract

Total Trail Miles (Certified): 8.1

Features: McCormick Wilderness includes 16,850 acres, or about 27 square miles of forested land and small scattered lakes. The area also contains the 3,675 acre McCormick Research Natural Area designated in 1971, and part of the Yellow Dog River, a river in the Wild and Scenic River system. The lay of the land at McCormick is varied, ranging from nearly level to rocky cliffs and outcroppings. The glacier-scoured hills of McCormick Wilderness are covered with a mixture of northern hardwood and lowland conifer forests that reclaimed the land after the logging era of the early 1900's. Animals that live in the area are typical of northern lake states forests and include white-tailed deer, black bear, otter, fox, mink, squirrels, and snowshoe hare. Bird watchers will find a variety including the loon and pileated woodpecker.

Local Information: Ottawa National Forest (Supervisor's Office) 906-932-1330 or 800-562-1201 (in Michigan) www.fs.fed.us/r9/ottawa/

Map Sources: NCTA, *Johnson - Marquette to Ironwood (M417A)*

Segment 37: Private Land

Range: Southwest boundary of McCormick Tract (Ottawa National Forest) to Craig Lake State Park. *(Note: This segment crosses private land.)*

Total Trail Miles (Certified): 4.0

Map Sources: NCTA, *Johnson - Marquette to Ironwood (M417A)*

Segment 38: Craig Lake State Park

Range: East park boundary (just north of West Branch Peshekee River) to west park boundary (northwest of Teddy Lake).

Total Trail Miles (Certified): 7.5

Features: Craig Lake State Park is the most remote state park in the system. It spans over 6,900 acres and is a wilderness area. The park contains six full lakes and numerous small ponds along with a variety of wildlife such as deer, black bear, beaver, loons, and a portion of the Upper Peninsula moose herd. Craig Lake is 374 acres and features six islands and high granite bluffs along its northern shoreline.

Local Information: Craig Lake State Park, 906-339-4461 www.michigandnr.com/parksandtrails/parksandtrailsinfo.asp?id=415

Map Sources: NCTA, *Johnson - Marquette to Ironwood (M417A)*

Segment 39: Copper Country State Forest

Range: Craig Lake State Park to southeast corner of Long Lake
Total Trail Miles: 1.1
Road Walk to Next Segment: 24.0 miles (not blazed)

Range: Southeast corner of Section 16 (south of Little Lake in Baraga Plains) to Ottawa National Forest Boundary at Forest Road 2233 *(Note: This segment crosses some private land.)*
Total Trail Miles: 12.1

Features: Flat to rolling sandy plains on State land, with numerous wetlands and abundant wildlife.

Local Volunteer Group: Peter Wolfe Chapter of NCTA
www.northcountrytrail.org/pwf/index.htm

Local Information: Copper Country State Forest, Michigan DNR (Marquette) 906-228-6561, www.michgan.gov/dnr/

Map Sources:
NCTA, *Alberta to Cascade Falls (MI-13)*
NCTA, *Hutchins Guidebook - NCT in Upper Michigan (M402)*

Segment 40: Ottawa National Forest

(Note: These segments cross some private land.)

Range: East boundary of the Ottawa National Forest at Forest Road 2233 to an access road (east of Victoria)
Total Trail Miles (Partially Certified): 46.2
Road Walk to Next Segment: 0.6 miles (not blazed)

Range: An access road (east of Victoria) to west boundary of Ottawa National Forest
Total Trail Miles (Partially Certified): 48.1

Features: The western half of the Forest has mainly rugged terrain with numerous cliff top overlooks, while the eastern half has rolling hills with numerous rivers and deep valleys. Yet the last 10 miles to the east is a sandy plain. The forest consists of mixed hardwoods and conifers, with occasional small wetlands.

Local Volunteer Group: Peter Wolfe Chapter of NCTA
www.northcountrytrail.org/pwf/index.htm

Local Information: Ottawa National Forest (Supervisor's Office)
906-932-1330 or 800-562-1201 (in Michigan) www.fs.fed.us/r9/ottawa/

Map Sources:
NCTA, *Alberta to Cascade Falls(MI-13) & Cascade Falls to Ironwood (MI-14)*
NCTA, *Hutchins Guidebook - NCT in Upper Michigan (M402)*
NCTA, *Johnson - Marquette to Ironwood (M417A)*

Lake of the Clouds
Photo by Aaron Phipps

Segment 41: Porcupine Mountains Wilderness State Park

Range: East Park boundary (southeast of Summit Peak Road) to County Road 519 *(Note: This segment crosses some private land.)*

Total Trail Miles (Partially Certified): 22.6

Features: The Park's 60,000 acres include towering virgin timber, secluded lakes, and miles of wild rivers and steams. This is one of the few remaining large wilderness areas in the Eastern United States.

Local Volunteer Group: Peter Wolfe Chapter of NCTA
www.northcountrytrail.org/pwf/index.htm

Local Information: Porcupine Mountains Wilderness State Park, 906-885-5275
www.michigandnr.com/parksandtrails/parksandtrailsinfo.asp?id=426

Map Sources:
NCTA, *Cascade Falls to Ironwood (MI-14)*
NCTA, *Hutchins Guidebook - NCT in Upper Michigan (M402)*
NCTA, *Johnson - Marquette to Ironwood (M417A)*

Segment 42: Ottawa National Forest

Range: County Road 519 to trailhead on Old 513 near Copper Peak Ski Flying Hill

Total Trail Miles (Certified): 11.8

Features: The trees are a hardwood mix with numerous rivers, cliff overlooks, deep valleys and spectacular waterfalls.

Local Information: Ottawa National Forest (Supervisor's Office) 906-932-1330 or 800-562-1201 (in Michigan), www.fs.fed.us/r9/ottawa/

Map Sources:
NCTA, *Cascade Falls to Ironwood (MI-14)*
NCTA, *Hutchins Guidebook - NCT in Upper Michigan (M402)*
NCTA, *Johnson - Marquette to Ironwood (M417A)*

Additional Information

For more information regarding lodging, other types of accommodations, or other general tourism information about the state of Michigan, try:
http://travel.michigan.org/
http://www.ring.com/travel/parks.htm
http://www.tourismcenter.msu.edu/
http://gorp.com/gorp/location/mi/mi.htm

For the Western half of Michigan, go to www.wmta.org or 800-442-2084 ext.110

Wisconsin

The trail enters Wisconsin from Upper Michigan near Hurley, possibly coming down historic and notorious Silver Street, though a final decision on the route across the state line has yet to be made. The first certified segment, known as the Uller Trail Segment, passes through Iron County Forest lands and offers many scenic overlooks. The trail route continues west along the Penokee-Gogebic Iron Range, ancient mountains worn away by glaciers and time, picking up the next completed segment at gorgeous Copper Falls State Park. The trail runs south through the park, down to the city of Mellen, and west to the Chequamegon-Nicolet National Forest.

In the forest, the trail continues along the Penokee-Gogebic Range with many rock outcroppings and scenic overlooks. It travels westward passing many wetlands, streams, and glacial lakes en route to the Marengo River and the old Swedish homestead with some of the most beautiful views in the forest. As the trail moves west through the Porcupine Lake and Rainbow Lake wilderness areas, the hills become gentler and the lakes more prevalent.

The trail enters the Bayfield County Forest and passes several nice, remote kettle lakes. Next is the Brule River State Forest where significant portions of the trail follow the rim of steep hillsides and the hiker will encounter a series of expansive vistas overlooking the valley of the famous Bois Brule River. The last 2 ½ miles running south though the Brule River State Forest follow the Historic Brule-St. Croix Portage. Once used by Native Americans, early European explorers, and fur traders, this ancient path crosses the Eastern Continental Divide and connects Lake Superior with the Mississippi River via these two famous rivers. Just south of the portage, the trail continues through the village of Solon Springs and Lucius Woods County Park. Heading west towards Minnesota, no trail exists except for a couple miles through Pattison State Park.

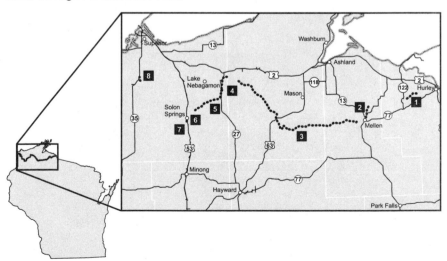

Segment 1: Uller Trail (Iron County Forest)

Range: Junction with snowmobile trail #6 just west of Valley Road (north of Iron Belt) to trailhead near Weber Lake on County Road E

Total Trail Miles (Certified): 5.1

Features: Pass through the Penokee Mountains, the oldest mountains in the area

Local Volunteer Group: Heritage Chapter of NCTA, www.northcountrytrail.org/htg/

Local Information: Hurley Chamber of Commerce, 715-561-4334

Map Sources:
NCTA, *Ironwood to Long Mile Lookout (WI-01)*
NCTA, *Hutchins Guidebook - NCT through Wisconsin (M501A)*

Segment 2: Copper Falls State Park through City of Mellen

Range: Sandstone ledges on north side of park to west edge of Mellen on Kornstead Road *(Note: This segment crosses some private land.)*

Total Trail Miles (Certified): 6.6

Features: Bad and Tyler Forks Rivers join and form spectacular waterfalls

Local Volunteer Group: Heritage Chapter of NCTA, www.northcountrytrail.org/htg/
Chequamegon Chapter of NCTA, www.northcountrytrail.org/che/

Local Information: Mellen Chamber of Commerce, 715-274-2330

Copper Falls State Park, 715-274-5123
www.dnr.state.wi.us/org/land/parks/specific/findapark.html#copfalls

Map Sources:
NCTA, *Ironwood to Long Mile Lookout (WI-01)*
NCTA, *Hutchins Guidebook - NCT through Wisconsin (M501A)*

Road Walk to Next Segment: 1.9 miles (blazed)

Copper Falls State Park
Photo by Bill Menke

Chequamegon National Forest
Photo by Tana Turonie

Segment 3: Chequamegon National Forest

Range: From trailhead at Kornstead Road to Chequamegon National Forest/
Bayfield County Forest Boundary (east of Bayfield County Highway A)

Total Trail Miles (Certified): 61.1

Features: May spot an elk or two, vista overlooking Marengo River Valley, two
wilderness areas, many small lakes and streams

Local Volunteer Group:
Chequamegon Chapter of NCTA, www.northcountrytrail.org/che/

Local Information: Chequamegon National Forest
Washburn Ranger District 715-373-2667 www.fs.fed.us/r9/cnnf/
Hayward Office of the Great Divide 715-634-4821, www.fs.fed.us/r9/cnnf/
Glidden Ranger District 715-264-2511, www.fs.fed.us/r9/cnnf/

Map Sources:
NCTA, *Ironwood to Long Mile Lookout (WI-01)*
NCTA, *Long Mile Lookout to Solon Springs (WI-02)*
NCTA, *Hutchins Guidebook - NCT through Wisconsin (M501A)*

Segment 4: Bayfield County Forest

Range: Bayfield County Forest/Chequamegon National Forest boundary (east of Bayfield Co Hwy A) to Wills Road

Total Trail Miles (Partially Certified): 9.6 miles

Local Volunteer Group:
Chequamegon Chapter of NCTA, www.northcountrytrail.org/che/
Brule-St.Croix Chapter of NCTA, www.northcountrytrail.org/bsc/

Local Information: Bayfield County Forest, 715-373-6114

Map Sources:
NCTA, *Long Mile Lookout to Solon Springs (WI-02)*

Segment 5: Brule River State Forest

Range: County Line Road to Douglas County Hwy A

Total Trail Miles (Certified): 21.7

Features: Large areas of red and white pines. Trail parallels Brule River

Local Volunteer Group: Brule-St.Croix Chapter, NCTA
www.northcountrytrail.org/bsc/

Local Information: Brule River State Forest, 715-372-5678
www.dnr.state.wi.us/org/land/Forestry/StateForests/meet.htm#BruleRiver

Map Sources:
NCTA, *Long Mile Lookout to Solon Springs (WI-02)*
NCTA, *Hutchins Guidebook - NCT through Wisconsin (M501A)*

Road Walk to Next Segment: 3.0 miles (blazed)

Brule River State Forest
Photo by Bill Menke

Segment 6: Village of Solon Springs (North Segment)

Range: Intersection of Co. Rd. A and E. Third street through Lucius Woods County Park in the middle of the village to Village Park Ave.

Total Trail Miles (Certified): 2.0

Features: Lucius Woods County Park

Local Volunteer Group: Brule-St.Croix Chapter of NCTA
www.northcountrytrail.org/bsc/

Map Sources:
NCTA, *Long Mile Lookout to Solon Springs (WI-02)*
NCTA, *Hutchins Guidebook - NCT through Wisconsin (M501A)*

Road Walk to Next Segment: 0.2 mile (not blazed)

Segment 7: Village of Solon Springs (South Segment)

Range: Old Hwy 53 to new Hwy 53

Total Trail Miles (Certified): 0.7

Local Volunteer Group: Brule-St.Croix Chapter of NCTA
www.northcountrytrail.org/bsc/

Map Sources:
NCTA, *Long Mile Lookout to Solon Springs (WI-02)*
NCTA, *Hutchins Guidebook - NCT through Wisconsin (M501A)*

Road Walk to Next Segment: 20 miles (blazed)

Segment 8: Pattison State Park

Range: South Boundary to jct State Road 35 and park entrance

Total Trail Miles (Certified): 2.8

Features: Big Manitou Falls which is the highest waterfall in Wisconsin

Local Volunteer Group: Brule-St.Croix Chapter of NCTA
www.northcountrytrail.org/bsc/

Local Information: Pattison State Park, 715-399-3111
www.dnr.state.wi.us/org/land/parks/specific/pattison

Additional Information

For more information regarding lodging, other types of accommodations, or other general tourism information about the state of Wisconsin, try:
www.wisconsin.com or www.travelwisconsin.com

Minnesota

Rivers, lakes and forest characterize the North Country Trail through much of its route in Minnesota. The terrain is often hilly and occasionally rugged. The northeastern Arrowhead region follows the dramatic shoreline of Lake Superior and part of the Boundary Waters Canoe Area. The forest cover is spruce and pine with maples on the ridges. In the middle of the state the forest cover includes mixed oak, maple, and aspen forest and some remains of the tall pine forests. In the west there is more farmland, a bit of prairie and the flat Red River delta. Surprising bluffs and overlooks appear when least expected.

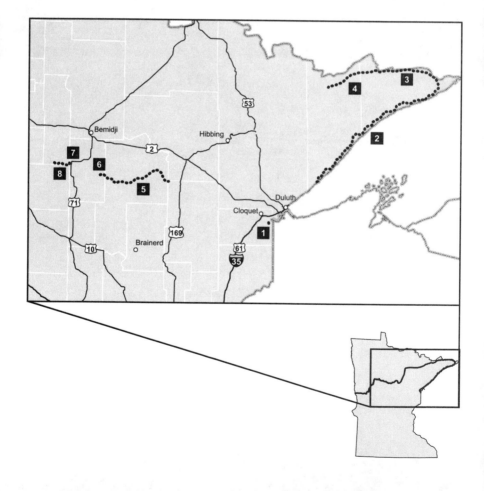

Superior Hiking Trail
Photo by Superior Hiking Trail Association

Segment 1: Jay Cooke State Park

Range: South end of Bearchase Loop to north end of the Swinging Bridge

Total Trail Miles (Certified): 3.1

Features: Water eroded gorge of the St. Louis River

Local Volunteer Group: Star of North Chapter of NCTA
www.northcountrytrail.org/stn/index.htm

Local Information: Jay Cooke State Park
218-384-4610, www.dnr.state.mn.us/state_parks/jay-cooke/index.html

Road Walk to Next Segment: 50 miles (not blazed)

Segment 2: Superior Hiking Trail

Total Trail Miles: 235

Features: Ascents to rock outcroppings and cliffs, descents into numerous creek and river valleys, spectacular waterfall, rapids and deep gorges

Partner Contact: Superior Hiking Trail Association, 218-834-2700, www.shta.org

Map Sources:
SHTA, *The Guide to the Superior Hiking Trail**
SHTA, *Map 1 - Two Habors to Tettegouche**
SHTA, *Map 2 - Tettegouche to Oberg Mt**
SHTA, *Map 3 - Oberg Mt to Woods Creek**
SHTA, *Map 4 - Woods Creek to Canada**

Road Walk to Next Segment: 0.2 mile (not blazed)

Segment 3: Border Route Trail

Total Trail Miles: 65.4

Features: Numerous overlooks of Canada, Bridalveil Falls and some old growth pine forests.

Partner Contact: Rovers Outing Club, www.mnrovers.org

Local Information: Superior National Forest
218-626-4300, www.superiornationalforest.org/

Map Sources:
Rovers Outing Club, *The Border Route Trail - A Trail Guide and Map***
Rovers Outing Club, *Map 1 - Gunflint Trail to Loon Lake***
Rovers Outing Club, *Map 2 - Loon Lake Road to South Lake Trail***
Rovers Outing Club, *Map 3 -South Lake Trail to Rove Lake***
Rovers Outing Club, *Map 4 -Rove Lake to West Pike Lake***
Rovers Outing Club, *Map 5 - West Pike Lake to McFarland Lake***
Rovers Outing Club, *Map 6 - McFarland Lake to Stump River***
Rovers Outing Club, *Map 7- Stump River to Partridge Falls***
Rovers Outing Club, *Map 8- Partridge Falls to Grand Portage***

Road Walk to Next Segment: 0.4 mile (not blazed)

Segment 4: Kekekabic Trail

Total Trail Miles: 35.0

Features: Heart of the Boundary Waters with deep woods and challenging terrain.

Partner Contact: Kekekabic Trail Club, 800-818-4453, www.kek.org

Local Information: Superior National Forest
218-626-4300, www.superiornationalforest.org/

Map Sources:
McKenzie Maps, *The Hikers BWCA Wilderness Companion: Kekekabic Trail Guide****
McKenzie Maps, *Maps 7,8,9****

Road Walk to Next Segment: 175 miles (not blazed)

Segment 5: Chippewa National Forest

Total Trail Miles (Certified): 71.9

Features: Wetlands, lakes and steams skirt the third largest lake in Minnesota and the home of the largest concentration of bald eagles in the US.

Local Volunteer Group: Star of North Chapter of NCTA
www.northcountrytrail.org/stn/index.htm

Local Information: Chippewa National Forest
218-335-8600, www.fs.fed.us/r9/chippewa/

Map Sources:
NCTA, *Chippewa National Forest to Paul Bunyan State Forest (MN-09)*
NCTA, *Hutchins Guidebook - NCT Through Minnesota's Chippewa National Forest and Itasca State Park (M601)*

Segment 6: Paul Bunyan State Forest

Range: Chippewa National Forest Boundary to Akeley Cutoff

Total Trail Miles (Partially Certified): 8.5

Features: Steep hills, moraine, potholes and is still a working forest

Local Volunteer Group: Itasca Moraine Chapter of NCTA
www.northcountrytrail.org/itm/index.htm

Local Information: Paul Bunyan State Forest
218-732-3309, www.dnr.state.mn.us/state_forests/sft00038/index.html

Road Walk to Next Segment: 25 miles (not blazed)

Segment 7: Itasca State Park

Range: Hwy 200 near east entrance to W. Park Boundary

Total Trail Miles (Certified): 13.0

Features: Headwaters of Mississippi River and Aiton Tower for climbing

Local Information: Itasca State Park
218 266-2100, www.dnr.state.mn.us/state_parks/itasca/index.html

Map Sources: NCTA, *Hutchins Guidebook - NCT Through Minnesota's Chippewa National Forest and Itasca State Park (M601)*

Segment 8: Bad Medicine – Clearwater County Forest

Range: Itasca State Park to Old Headquarters Site, Clearwater County Road 39

Total Trail Miles (Partially Certified): 7.3

Features: Hilly terrain, potholes and small lakes

Local Volunteer Group: Itasca Moraine Chapter of NCTA
www.northcountrytrail.org/itm/index.htm

Local Information: Clearwater County Forest, 218-694-6227

Map Sources: Currently no maps available

Additional Information

* To order map from the Superior Hiking Trail Association please contact them by phone at 218-834-2700, or visit their Web site at www.shta.org.

** To order map from the Rovers Outing Club please visit their Web site at www.mnrovers.org.

*** To order map from McKenzie Maps please contact them by phone at 800-749-2113, or visit their Web site at www.mckenziemaps.com..

For more information regarding lodging, other types of accommodations, or other general tourism information about the state of Minnesota, try:

www.exploreminnesota.com

Minnesota Department of Tourism, 888-868-7476

North Dakota

Throughout North Dakota, trail users will thrill to see flocks of geese, ducks, and sandhill cranes as they traverse the scenery of our northern prairies. North Dakota is a land of wide-open spaces and the sky dominates everywhere you look. There is nothing to compare to watching a prairie thunderstorm move across the landscape or the star lit Dakota night sky. The trail in ND travels from the ancient lakebed of glacial lake Agassiz to the rolling prairie pothole region to the Missouri River basin through tall and mixed grass prairies. From the Minnesota state line, the trail route continues westward to Fort Abercrombie State Historic Site and the Red River Valley. Hikers will enjoy the segment in Sheyenne National Grassland – a 71,000-acre remnant of a tall grass prairie. The trail follows the Sheyenne River's scenic forested valley northward to Sheyenne State Forest and Fort Ransom State Park. The trail continues northward along the Sheyenne River Valley to Lake Ashtabula and on to Fort Totten State Historic site near Devils Lake. The trail follows along the Garrison Diversion Project Canals and then continues along the shores of Audubon and Lake Sakakawea. The Lonetree segment of the trail may be more difficult to hike because of its vegetation and terrain. The trail is not groomed, but simply a delineated route. When passing through the Lonetree segment of the trail, a hiker can expect to see a variety of habitat including wetlands, native prairie and grasslands. Wildlife such as sharp-tailed grouse, ring-necked pheasants, Hungarian partridges and white-tailed deer can also be seen when hiking through Lonetree. Three primitive campgrounds are situated along the Lonetree segment of the North Country Trail and each offers drinking water, vault toilets and picnic tables.

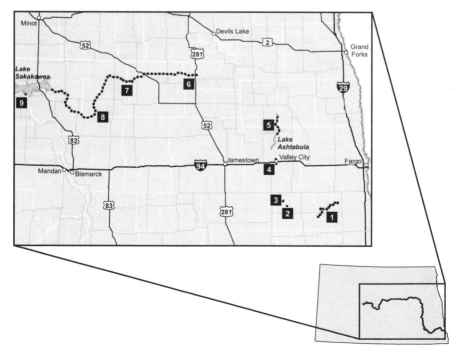

Segment 1: Sheyenne National Grassland

Range: Trail begins 1.2 miles northeast of Richland County Road 23 and continues to a dirt road east of Iron Springs Creek
Total Trail Miles (Certified): 9.3
Road Walk to Next Segment: 0.1 mile (not blazed)

Range: Dirt road east of Iron Springs Creek to Ransom County Road 54/141st Avenue SE
Total Trail (Certified): 23.8
Road Walk to Next Segment: 27 miles (not blazed)

Features: Restoration of tallgrass prairie, rare white fringed orchid, prairie chicken, moose, wolves and two unique butterfly species

Local Information: Sheyenne National Grassland (Sheyenne Ranger District) 701-683-4342, www.fs.fed.us/r1/dakotaprairie/sheyenne.htm

Map Sources:
NTCA, *North Dakota Special Edition (ND-SE)*
NTCA, *Hutchins Guidebook - NCT In North Dakota (M701)*

Sheyenne National Grassland
Photo by Ken Howell

Segment 2: Sheyenne State Forest

Range: Follows nature hiking trail. Trailhead is off 122nd Ave SE

Total Trail Miles (Certified): 0.7

Features: Slopes and ravines as well as open and wooded areas

Local Information: North Dakota Forest Service, 701-683-4323,
www.ndsu.nodak.edu/ndsu/lbakken/forest/stateforest/sheyenne.htm

Map Sources: NTCA, *North Dakota Special Edition (ND-SE)*

Road Walk to Next Segment: 6 miles (not blazed)

Segment 3: Fort Ransom State Park

Total Trail Miles (Certified): 1.9

Features: West bank of Sheyenne River Basin, demonstration farm, wooded and open fields

Local Information: Fort Ransom State Park
701-973-433, www.ndparks.com/parks/FRSP.htm

Map Sources: NTCA, *North Dakota Special Edition (ND-SE)*

Road Walk to Next Segment: 30 miles (not blazed)

Lonetree Wildlife Management Area
Photo by Garrison Diversion, Will Kincaid

Segment 4: Valley City

Range: South of Valley City on Barnes County Road 21 (117th Street SE) to 9th Avenue NW on north side of Valley City

Total Trail Miles (Certified): 4.6

Features: Scenic overlooks, Indian burial mounds, Medicine Wheel Park and North Dakota's City of Bridges

Local Volunteer Group: Sheyenne River Valley Chapter of NTCA www.northcountrytrail.org/srv/index.htm

Local Information: Valley City Chamber of Commerce 701-845-1891, www.hellovalley.com/valleycity/treasures/chamber.html

Map Sources: NTCA, *North Dakota Special Edition (ND-SE)*

Road Walk to Next Segment: 17 miles (not blazed)

Segment 5: Lake Ashtabula

Range: West Ashtabula Crossing at Barnes County Road 21 to North end of COE ownership near 5th Street SE

Total Trail Miles (Certified): 16.9

Features: Grassland, hills, fields and lake. Includes water management areas

Local Volunteer Group: Sheyenne River Valley Chapter of NTCA www.northcountrytrail.org/srv/index.htm

Local Information: US Army Corps of Engineers, Lake Ashtabula Project Office 701-845-2970

Map Sources: NTCA, *North Dakota Special Edition (ND-SE)*

Road Walk to Next Segment: 80 miles (not blazed)

Segment 6: New Rockford Canal

Range: 1 mile east of State Road 2812 to Lonetree Wildlife Management Area

Total Trail Miles (Certified): 41.0

Features: Mostly rolling farmland and pasture

Local Information: Bureau of Reclamation (Garrision Diversion Conservancy District) 800-532-0074, www.garrisondiv.org

Map Sources: NTCA, *Hutchins Guidebook - NCT In North Dakota (M701)*

Lake Sakakawea State Park
Photo by Aaron Phipps

Segment 7: Lonetree Wildlife Management Area

Range: New Rockford Canal to McClusky Canal

Total Trail Miles (Certified): 32.0

Features: A diverse range of habitats, wetlands, native prairie and grassland

Local Volunteer Group: Lonetree Chapter of NTCA
www.northcountrytrail.org/ltr/index.htm

Local Information: North Dakota Game and Fish Department
701-324-2211, www.state.nd.us/gnf

Bureau of Reclamation (Garrision Diversion Conservancy District)
800-532-0074, www.garrisondiv.org

Map Sources: NTCA, *Hutchins Guidebook - NCT In North Dakota (M701)*

Segment 8: McClusky Canal

Range: Lonetree Management Area to Lake Audubon spillway

Total Trail Miles (Certified): 74.0

Features: All types of wildlife, agricultural and native prairie landscape, a series of lakes in line with the canal, as well as canal features including a pumping station.

Local Information: Bureau of Reclamation (Garrision Diversion Conservancy District)
800-532-0074, www.garrisondiv.org

Map Sources: NTCA, *Hutchins Guidebook - NCT In North Dakota (M701)*

Road Walk to Next Segment: 22 miles (not blazed)

Segment 9: Lake Sakakawea State Park

Range: The park is located off Highway 200

Total Trail Miles (Certified): 1.0

Features: Largest man-made reservoir in the nation.

Local Information: Lake Sakakawea State Park
701-487-3315, www.ndparks.com/parks/lssp.htm

Map Sources: NTCA, *Hutchins Guidebook - NCT In North Dakota (M701)*

Additional Information

For more information regarding lodging, other types of accommodations, or other general tourism information about the state of North Dakota visit: www.northdakota.com

History

The National Trails System Act, first passed in 1968, established the Appalachian and Pacific Crest Trails as the nation's first National Scenic Trails. The Act also identified several additional trails for study, including the North Country National Scenic Trail. A committee composed of federal, state, local and private sector representatives was formed in each state potentially affected by the NCT to recommend a route for the trail. The final conceptual study report, published in June 1975, identified a 10-mile wide planning corridor. The study concluded that the route met the criteria for National Scenic Trails, and an amendment to the Act authorized the North Country National Scenic Trail on March 5, 1980.

In the late 1970s, Lance Feild united several volunteers that were interested in the concept of the North Country Trail, and the passage of the legislation in 1980 moved him to action to form the North Country Trail Association. He arranged for the NCTA to receive an abandoned schoolhouse in White Cloud, Michigan, for its headquarters, and it was here that the NCTA held its first meeting in 1980.

Meanwhile, the Midwest Region of the National Park Service took on federal responsibility for the trail. Working without specific funding for the trail, two NPS employees took on the massive challenge of completing a Comprehensive Plan. This required hosting planning meetings in all the trail's states and corresponding with more than 1,000 affected parties. Once its Congressional obligation to complete the trail was fulfilled, the NPS was persuaded to keep one staff person in place to coordinate ongoing work on the NCT and two other trails. An advisory council, established by the 1980 legislation, worked during this time to seek support from state governments and set early direction for implementation of the comprehensive plan, while the NCTA itself began to grow.

Throughout the 1980s, the North Country Trail Association continued to grow. In these years, membership slowly increased, and many private individuals made significant contributions through trail building and maintenance, event planning, and regular attendance at meetings. During this period, the NCTA had but one chapter, the Western Michigan Chapter, near Grand Rapids, Michigan.

1990 brought a great watershed for the NPS in its relationship with the trail. The NPS opened a separate trails office in Madison, Wisconsin, to serve the NCT, the Ice Age National Scenic Trail, and the Lewis and Clark National Historic Trail. Under NPS staff guidance, work on the trail increased steadily and, in 1992, the NPS added it's first full-time position to be solely dedicated to the trail. During this period, the NCTA and the NPS negotiated a Cooperative Agreement, which provided NPS funding to the NCTA and led to the hiring of the Association's first executive director. In addition, NPS Challenge Cost Share funding also began to directly support trail projects. By 1991, just short of 1,000 miles of trail had been certified. In a decade, much had been accomplished, but potential trail projects on public lands were getting increasingly scarce.

As the trail evolved in the mid-1990s, the Association evolved along with it, shifting from a small trail club to a major trail overseer with national responsibilities.

Along with this, the Association was one of the key players in the development of the Partnership for the National Trails System. As the Partnership has developed, NCTA has taken a leadership role in many functions, including efforts to influence federal legislation and regulatory efforts pertaining to the trail community.

Another development aimed at the dwindling amount of public lands available for trail expansion was the creation of a Land Trust Fund for the purchase of easements or titles of critical pieces of land. The Land Trust Fund was given its initial start in 1994 with memorial donations for Alfred E. Borsum, a Middleville, Michigan, businessman.

Development of regional chapters of the NCTA was another focus during this period. A core group of four Chapters expanded dramatically to the NCTA's current roster of more than two dozen Chapters. By 1997, limited representation of the growing list of Chapters on the NCTA Board led to a reorganization involving the formation of regional Trail Councils. Today, seven Trail Councils coordinate the work of Chapters and other partners, offering a strong regional focus on trail development and management.

The NCTA hired a recreation planner, stationed in the Madison Office of the NPS, and expanded its Executive Director position to full-time by the end of 1996.

In the late 1990s, the NCTA improved its newsletter and set up its first Web site, to more effectively spread the word about the trail. These efforts paid off, as membership topped the 1,000 mark for the first time in mid-1998, at least partly a reflection of the intense growth in chapters and local support. By the end of 2002, membership had topped 2,800.

With the growth of the NCTA came new programs and services. The most significant of these was the start of a geographic information system (GIS) effort in 1997. Initially run by an intern and existing staff, the GIS program expanded dramatically with funding from the Grand Rapids Community Foundation and the hiring of a full time cartographer in the fall of 2000. The NCTA's GIS program now produces many high quality maps for route planning, trail promotion and education, and, of course, hiking.

Partnerships with federal agencies and private organizations also continued to grow around the turn of the century. By 2001, the NCTA had Affiliate agreements with six independent nonprofit organizations that managed portions of the trail.

Expanding services at NCTA headquarters also caused the Association to finally outgrow its meager office in downtown Grand Rapids, Michigan. So, in the spring of 2001, the NCTA relocated to a storefront in the historic district of Lowell, Michigan, just one block from the trail itself. With the addition of a new Director of Trail Management in late 2002, the NCTA is poised to dramatically expand up on its successful history of building, maintaining, protecting and promoting the North Country National Scenic Trail.